Islam

In Translation: Modern Muslim Thinkers

Series Editor: Abdou Filali-Ansary

Books in the series include

Islam:
Between Message and History
Abdelmadjid Charfi

Islam and the Foundations of Political Power
Ali Abdelraziq

Governance from the Perspective of Islam
Ayatullah Aqa Sheikh Muhammad Hussein Na'ini
With a Commentary by
Ayatullah Sayyid Mahmud Taleqani

Islam

Between Message and History

ABDELMADJID CHARFI

Translated by
David Bond

Edited by
Abdou Filali-Ansary
and Sikeena Karmali Ahmed

EDINBURGH UNIVERSITY PRESS
IN ASSOCIATION WITH

THE AGA KHAN UNIVERSITY
INSTITUTE FOR THE STUDY OF MUSLIM CIVILISATIONS

Note on transliteration
For transliteration of non-Latin script we have used as far as
possible the IJMES system. Original Arabic and Persian titles
of reference works can be found in the endnotes. All words foreign
to the English language have been italicised.

The opinions expressed in this volume are those of the authors
and do not necessarily reflect those of the Aga Khan University,
Institute for the Study of Muslim Civilisations.

© Abdelmadjid Charfi, 2003
Introduction © Moncef Ben Abdeljelil, 2009
English translation © David Bond, 2009

Edinburgh University Press Ltd
22 George Square, Edinburgh

Typeset in Garamond Premier
by Koinonia, Manchester, and
printed and bound in Great Britain
by CPI Antony Rowe, Chippenham and Eastbourne

A CIP record for this book is available
from the British Library

ISBN 978 0 7486 3967 0 (hardback)

Contents

Introduction

MONCEF BEN ABDELJELIL

Abdelmadjid Charfi, the author of this book (published in the English translation under the auspices of the Aga Khan University, Institute for the Study of Muslim Civilisations in London), is one of the most outstanding researchers in the field of religious studies and Islamic thought. He is one of a few thinkers distinguished for their deep insight, their rigorous methodology and their sound analysis. His accurate interpretation is grounded in detailed knowledge of the original sources and careful reading of contemporary insights in the humanities and sociology. Charfi has closely followed developments in this wide and complex field with its multiple perspectives – and many potential pitfalls.

Abdelmadjid Charfi was born in the Tunisian city of Sfax in 1942 and initially attended a Qur'anic school before going to the Sadikia secondary school in Tunis, where a programme of modern education was inaugurated in both French and Arabic. Tunisian reformist and modernising thought developed within this school, which also nurtured the elite who led the new, independent Tunisia and founded its educational, legislative and cultural institutions. Abdelmadjid Charfi belonged to the first generation of students at the Higher Institute for Teacher Training in Tunis, one of the most important institutes of higher education, founded along the lines of the École Normale Supérieure in Paris. This rigorous intellectual training enabled Charfi to pursue his studies in France. After graduating with distinction from the Sorbonne he taught at the University of Tunis.

During the 1970s, the domain of "Civilisation Studies" was a nebulous one, with the exception of the sterling efforts of a few outstanding scholars such as Ahmed Abdessalam, Mohamed Talbi, Farhat Dachraoui and Hichem Djaït. Charfi was a contemporary of this group and followed the development of their thought. It was inevitable that he, on the basis of his learning and research, should propel Arabic studies toward the development of a specialised field of study still known today as "Civilisation Studies". In this area Charfi was a pioneer and a founder in the full sense of the term, establishing a discipline whose premises and results were coherent, and which drew in a critical manner on the approach of the human and social sciences in their various branches. Civilisation Studies was thus able to occupy a distinct position among other established scholarly disciplines. Civilisation Studies drew on religious anthropology, as well as Muslim disciplines, history and human geography, the wide spectrum of human science, sociology, philosophy and linguistics, as well as knowledge of the Arabic language.

Abdelmadjid Charfi's varied scholarship has been based on a comparative examination of, on the one hand, the meaning of the message of Muhammad in its original setting of seventh-century Arabia, and the subsequent reception of this message by generations of Muslims and non-Muslims alike. Questions that he has studied include, for example, Muslim views of Christianity, as well as the structure of the arguments that Muslims developed following the revelation of the Qur'anic texts, the Bible, Qur'anic exegesis and dogma. This comparison between original meaning and subsequent reception is also evident in his work on the theme of Islam and modernity, whether it be current trends within Islam or Charfi's call for the necessary nurturing of an enlightened conscience, integrating the tenets of religion, universal humanity and the values of modernity. Charfi's approach goes beyond Islam, encompassing the phenomenon of religion from its beginnings, its subsequent development and evolving meaning, giving as examples both adherents and opponents of religion.

It is noteworthy that Charfi considers religion as a phenomenon that can be examined and studied, one that has meanings and functions for its adherents, throughout its history. The only way to study these is in the light of laws governing the history of civilisation. Religious scholarship shakes off the grip of repetition and marginal glosses and opens up to renewal based on novel and creative thought. Charfi's enquiry covers the whole of the Islamic tradition, promoting deeper understanding and attitudes conducive to personal lucidity and responsibility, in harmony with contemporary values.

Introduction

On the basis of this view of Islam, Charfi has published a number of books and essays, and edited a series of publications about the renewal of Islamic thought, including *Muslim Thought and Its Response to Christians Until the End of the Fourth/Tenth Century* (Tunis/Algiers, 1986), *Islam and Modernity* (Tunis: Dār al tunisiyya lil nashr, 1990), *A Renewal of Islamic Thought* (Casablanca: Fennec Editions, 1998), *Islam: Between Message and History* (Beirut: Dār et Talī'a, 2001) and *Islamic Thought: Rupture and Continuity* (Tunis: Dār el Janoub/Paris: Albin Michel, 2008).

This series of publications edited by Charfi represents a personal project of research and study. It was also a way of associating younger scholars with his work and reflection, while also becoming a testing ground for research methods which he has applied to various subjects. Sixteen titles have appeared in a series called "Islam Singular and Plural", studying cultural pluralism within a contextualised view of Islam. He has prepared the ground for a programme of research that will doubtless be enriched in the future. Charfi, despite his continuing creativity, had to retire from teaching when he was sixty. However, he has not withdrawn from university life or lost contact with students; he is still committed to directing and evaluating their work.

It is important to mention that Charfi has supervised numerous theses whose authors have followed in his footsteps and drawn inspiration from his capacity to identify the specificity of a particular question, his rigorous analytical approach as well as his personal commitment to learning and its advancement. The research of these younger scholars represents more than the title of an academic certificate: they have become part of Charfi's research project and the scholarly view he has evolved, one that developed from the work of innovative thinkers ill at ease amid the crisis of religious thought, the decline of religious learning in the Arab and Muslim worlds and the plagues of violent extremism and self-interest. There has been a corresponding loss of freedom and an undermining of the basic rights that guarantee intellectual creativity, individual responsibility, integrity and social vitality. Abdelmadjid Charfi has, therefore, sown a seed which will burgeon in the minds of a new generation of researchers, a sign of his belief in the universality of learning and his response to the contribution he received from the proponents of renewal, among his contemporaries and his predecessors.

Islam

In the Company of the Innovators

"Innovators" is a term with numerous meanings, some of which may be a source of confusion, a point that should be mentioned before proceeding further. One of the meanings handed down from the past is derived from a hadīth attributed to the Prophet, the so-called "hadīth of renewal" according to which God sends every hundred years a person who will renew the community's religion. This hadīth has been employed by plagiarists and falsifiers with two aims: to counter the concept of the Mahdi in Imami Shī'ism in particular, and as a subterfuge to dilute the negative associations of the term *bid'a*, associated with innovation and deviance, also mentioned in the hadīths attributed to the Prophet. It is certain that Charfi and his fellow innovative thinkers are not "hundred-year" emissaries or supporters of the Mahdi. They are creative thinkers who have developed a new way of looking at religion, one that sustains them in the face of tradition. Through their writings they have freed themselves and evolved a coherent system of thought pertinent to their world.

Renewal can also mean the revival and purification of religion, as used by Wahīd Khān in his book written in Urdu in 1978, entitled *The Renewal of the Religious Sciences*, although we do not consider that Charfi and his associates adhere to this view.

Charfi's viewpoint, on the contrary, is closer to that emerging from an article by Amīn al Khūli published in the review *Risāla* in 1933 with the title of "Renewal in Religion". Khūli embarks on a reexamination of the text of the Qur'an and narrative material associated with the Prophet, seen in the light of recently discovered data and today's needs. Built around sound logical analysis and discernment, renewal entails reconstructing, for today's world, an intellectual framework that is meaningful and functional, insofar as modernity models its basic constituents. Muhammad Iqbal (1877–1938) understood the term "renewal" as a rebuilding, the development of a new theory.

The position which Charfi has chosen is precisely that of the second Reform movement as mentioned by Abdou Filai-Ansari in his book *Réformer l'Islam.*[1] This reformism is not preoccupied with following the righteous ancestors; nor does it consider its mission as one of purifying religion and belief from "innovation" and plagues that have affected its unblemished spirit. From an intellectual point of view its task is clear: revising in a critical and rigorous way the structures of thought that preceding generations of scholars had put in place. The path that this reformism has chosen is not a secure and smooth road. It is a road that leads to the discovery of the values of the message of the Prophet in its Qur'anic form, translated by the Prophet into a form that took account of questions of history and actuality. This road also opens up the universal dimension of the Prophet's message. Thus, the principles of religion are a source of moral inspiration in the context of real history and the Muslim conscience is no longer divided. The reformers' project of revision is carried out in an intellectually rigorous way, pertinent to the time in which we live. This is a project different from that of the preceding generation, one that draws on the Islamic principle of legal capacity founded on freedom, maintaining a sense of responsibility which is an individual duty, not a collective one.

The basic change in the approach of the second Reform movement is one that goes beyond the question of identity, which Charfi considered a false question. The change consists in substituting a legalistic and insular religious structure with a moral pattern for living which realises the highest human creative capacities for the attainment of goodness and happiness.

A point of view such as that of Muhammad Iqbal concerning the perfection of prophecy should be situated against this kind of intellectual and theoretical background. Charfi drew on Iqbal's theory for inspiration when he declared to his interviewer in the review *Contemporary Islamic Questions* "the sealing of prophecy means that people become fully responsible without seeking outside advice, whatever justifications outside parties may present".[2] This is also the position of another contemporary Tunisian thinker, Mohamed Talbi (1923–) who, in his noteworthy defence of an "oriented reading" of the Qur'an, stated time and again that personal integrity, adoption of freedom as the basis of religion and the following of the moral and human aims of the Qur'an are all worthier and more important for the Muslim than following the ancestors and legislating according to their legal schools. Talbi called for *fiqh* (jurisprudence) to be set aside in favour of a new historical and spiritual approach in the light of the original aims of the Qur'an. This viewpoint is grounded in the insistence of the Pakistani thinker, Fazlur Rahman (1919–88) in *Islam and Modernity* on the necessity for the text of the Qur'an to be announced on the basis of a movement in two directions: the text is situated in the social and intellectual setting of seventh-century Arabia, so as to uncover the original meaning of the message and its general moral values. Moving on to today's realities, these values are translated into a form appropriate to the integration of believers in modern societies.

5

One may note that Fazlur Rahman likewise insists on the need to dispense with institutionalised legal scholarship and constraints imposed by theologians on the original aims of religion.

We do not subscribe to the generalisation that only Arab regions or scholars influenced by Orientalists are concerned by the radical reexamination of religion through the creation of a new interpretative method. The reality is very different. In Iran scholars such as Shaikh Muhammad Mujtahid Shabastari and Abdel Karim Sorush, though they may have differed in the application of their ideas and in their conclusions, do not deny the need to search for the moral aims of religion. Tradition can obscure the living text of the Qur'an, which is meaningful when situated in today's reality. By the standard of Iranian culture, Shabastari's book, *The Hermeneutics of the Qur'an and the Sunna*, is a highly significant text.

There are certain Indonesian thinkers who belong to the reformist school. They have been described, perhaps inaccurately, as the thinkers of "Liberal Islam". Among them are Nour Khalis Majīd and Abderrahman Wahid, and the current coordinator of the Liberal Islam Network, Ulil Abshar Abdalla, against whom Attia Ali, head of the Association of Indonesian 'Ulamā', issued a *fatwa* calling for him to be put to death following the publication of his article in the Indonesian newspaper, *Kompas Daily*, on 18 November 2002.

This small group of scholars base their reflection on the belief that there is no text which is somehow above interpretation when it is exposed to the conditions of modern life. Every text, including the Qur'an, has to be subjected to new interpretations and considered afresh. The same group of scholars lays down a second principle: the crucial point in a religious text is an understanding of its aim and its spirit, not the particular means through which this spirit was communicated in periods of history when prevailing mentality required such means. These thinkers have undertaken to safeguard the universal human principles of the text and create contemporary means of realising them. Some examples can illustrate the originality of their point of view. Nour Khalis Majīd, for example, holds that Islam is plural by necessity since it accepts variety as a social reality, beneficial for all. On this basis, Nour Khalis Majīd gives a novel interpretation of Sūra 3:19 which says, "God's religion is Islam", arguing that religion, any religion, is devotion to God and all religions are the same in this respect: Judaism, Christianity and Islam. He goes on to assert that: "Every believer who does good and is upright in heart and character is a spiritual Muslim. Along with Jews,

Christians and Magians, idol worshippers in India and China and Japan are also peoples of the Book and Muslims can marry their daughters." Ulil Abshar Abdalla shared this opinion, believing that positive values, wherever they are found, such as obedience and piety, are in fact Muslim values. All religions are equal in this respect. Ulil Abshar Abdalla adds that all forms of discrimination on grounds of religion and belief should disappear. Prevention of Muslims marrying non-Muslims is an interdiction that should disappear since the Qur'an considers people as equals, a single family whose members and inclinations vary and who seek and carry out the good in varying ways.

These thinkers, regardless of their origins in various parts of the Muslim world, share basic elements of this historical-critical approach that seeks liberation from traditional authority. This shows that the question of reform and the horizon of renewal are rooted in a modernity that is a limitless journey of discovery. This is the opposite to the traditional theological understanding of belief in Islam, as stated in the hadīth attributed to the Prophet: "The believer is like a camel: when he is curbed, he is led." The most important results of this research are particularly evident in the audacious practical applications carried out by some of these scholars.

Mohamed Talbi opposed the prevailing understanding of the Qur'anic text stipulating that women should be punished by beating, distancing himself from the ways in which jurists, when legislating, have considered women as inferior, to the point that discrimination against women has become an obstacle to development in the Muslim world. Fazlur Rahman, for his part, courageously opposed slavery although the Qur'an accepted it and legal scholars entrenched it on the basis of unjust (and disgraceful) judgments. His position on female inheritance has remained open to revision as a defence against the rancorous criticism directed against him, although he has not been entirely protected against it. Tunisian scholar Hichem Djaït was criticised for his refusal to accept that the story of the Cave had any significance; in his view it was a storyteller's invention.[3] Charfi has not hesitated to state clearly that fasting is not an obligation for Muslims as it is easy for them to substitute it with feeding the poor. This goes against the opinion of all the schools of jurisprudence and is contrary to popular belief, which is the basis for the authority of legal scholars, *muftis* (expounders of Muslim law), and, often, political rulers. This is the intellectual, theoretical and scholarly context of Abdelmadjid Charfi's book. It is a "building block" among many others similar to it, distinguished by its basis in the philosophy of human sciences as an instrument of examination and study. The premises of the book are governed by reason and fact. What has been the contribution of the human sciences, apart from the creation of a new approach among the members of the reformist group we have mentioned? Two essential elements can be identified: truth (of any kind) cannot be dissociated from the cultural context that nurtured it and from the structure of thought in the language that has fashioned the truth. Secondly, religion is one of the (many) phenomena through which culture communicates a possible way of understanding and structuring the place of human beings within existence (as it unfolds). As a consequence of the first important element, religious truth, traditionally thought to be far removed from people, though they might disagree about its nature, is seen as a truth in the course of elaboration through the efforts of those interpreting it. It is far from being the absolute truth formerly imagined. This is pertinent to the question that numerous scholars have endeavoured to examine, namely, the variety (and the pluralism) of Muslim cultures. The same quest structures the series of publications coordinated by Abdelmadjid Charfi, eloquently entitled *Islam: Singular and Plural.* The inevitable result is that religious knowledge founded by stories and accounts which have stabilised in the form of a seemingly fixed and eternal law have become the object of questioning and inquiry from outside the logical system sustaining it. Truth in the field of religion moved away from being a truth grounded in belief to a search for the way in which truth itself took form.

Such a search necessarily requires the questioning of articles of faith firmly established by a series of factors: the passage of time; an exaggerated attention to intellectual credibility; the sacrifice of the core moral values of religion; and a quest for legitimacy among the religious and political establishment.

How the humanities evaluate religion is a question with numerous ramifications. The central question concerns the way in which a religion takes on a specific form with meaningful structure in a society that adheres to this religion. There are three main elements in this system: the modes of belief; the characteristics of religious law; and the scale of moral values. This system is meaningful only if it explains the enigmas of human existence that perplex men and women. It is reasonable to maintain that the explanatory function is not created by the religion itself; rather, it is the religious person in an historical setting with the intellectual equipment furnished by his or her culture. The humanities illustrate how societies are capable, in a practical sense, of reinventing the interiorised or culturally defined explanatory approaches. These latter may appear venerable through the passing of the years and their retelling. In this setting Abdelmadjid Charfi presents *Islam: Between Message and History.*

A Title and a Vision

The title that Abdelmadjid Charfi has chosen for his book is one that opens up a question. The term "Islam" shifts from its stable position in culture, heritage and tradition (a position of power controlling belief and education) to become a phenomenon, thereby susceptible to historical examination and study. The proof of this change can be found in the author's move away from narrative knowledge to knowledge in the form of investigation and careful study. Knowledge as narration remains as the ancestors saw it: correct and valid knowledge, truth accepted in the name of belief, imitating the preexisting code of practice. Knowledge as questioning is a quest for understanding, to employ Hichem Djaït's term in *Revelation and the Qur'an and Prophecy* published in 2000. The usages of the past are the object of radical reexamination, and the validity of its results depends on the conclusions of the source criticism and the examination of these usages in the light of the laws of history and civilisation. For this to happen, the use of the human sciences has to be accepted as legitimate.

The title sets face to face two visions of Islam which are not similar, contrary to what Muslims thought for many decades. The first is a vision fashioned by the aims of the message, a living and growing discourse, in Muhammad's social context. The second is a vision of Islam current in history, among the successors to the first Muslim communities in cities and in successive eras of history, in a variety of societies with their cultures and questions. The title is eloquent through its use of the separation or bridge-word "between" to indicate the interpretative effort to which the message has been subjected in order to regulate the life of Muslims and promote religion with its explanatory role in different societies. Interestingly, the title also alludes to the way in which the interpreter approaches or distances himself from the aims of the message, claiming nevertheless that religion is being safeguarded. Charfi concentrates on the wide gulf or even contradiction between the original aim and the ways in which Muslims have interpreted it.

An example of this would be the Qur'anic call for liberty and the way that legal scholars entrenched slavery and gave details of judgments on the subject, the laying down of the principle of equality between the sexes and the persist-ently negative view of women to which legal scholars gave their seal of approval through a series of unfair practical provisions. Charfi intended that his readers should revise the essentialist view of Islam anchored in popular consciousness, and, through many examples, to study the Qur'an in its original social and intel-lectual setting.

He also examines the ways in which immediate challenges were handled, although the message transcends these, attaining a wider human dimension. Subsequent generations of Muslims imagined that through their religious heritage they were applying the teachings of Islam as they were revealed to Muhammad. Charfi's invitation (eloquently summarised in the title) to revisit all these questions is a quest for a reliable intellectual approach which can identify the moral core within the message of Islam, and which answers the dilemma of human conscience consumed by despair, without a moral element of restraint.

The title thus goes beyond the content of the book, enunciating an approach valid to questions beyond those concerning Islam. The title delineates the main sections of the book and its main points: the message of Islam in its original setting, its characteristics and organisation and the message in history, as well as a variety of questions which have been subject to interpretation by Muslims over time.

The Message of Islam: Closure of Prophecy "From the Outside"

Charfi examines the message of Islam through two phenomena: the Qur'an and the Prophet Muhammad. Charfi is aware of the intellectual difficul-ties associated with the historico-critical method in analysing religious texts, which have been assumed by a community, celebrated and revised, assembled and codified after a period of oral transmission. They have become a possession of the community through which God is worshipped. The phenomenon of Muhammad has also been enveloped in a mass of stories, legends and tales of the Prophet's military campaigns. These subsequent ways of imagining the Prophet were honest by the standards of their authors and their ways of expressing themselves. Their accounts of the Prophet's miracles furnish ample proof of this. The Qur'an clearly rejected that any miracle other than the eloquence of the Qur'an be associated with the Prophet. The Qur'an's origins were divine and the Prophet was not its source.

Charfi presents the research on the specificities of the message by highlighting the function of religion as a means of explaining the enigmas of human existence. This is an important dimension of the way in which people organise themselves in society and interact with its culture. It is striking that humans create institutions and subsequently confer religious sanctity upon them. The origins of these institutions are forgotten and they become religious absolutes (*Islam: Between Message and History*, page 29). The choice of 'Arafāt as the place where pilgrims spend the ninth day of the pilgrimage is a departure from the practice during the pilgrimage of Quraysh known as the pilgrimage of *al Hums*. This was for a political aim, that of weakening the power of Muhammad's Qurayshi opponents and also uniting followers, who would subsequently be termed the *Umma* or Muslim community.

For specialists of jurisprudence the question had been formalised and they argued unhesitatingly that the "Hajj is 'Arafāt". The same happened with regard to circumcision and the veil, which regrettably has become a major subject of debate between Muslims themselves and among non-Muslims. The fact of the matter is that Assyrian laws and Christian religious literature linked the veil to the social status of women.[4] Charfi examines the explanatory function of the two phenomena, Muhammad and the Qur'an, within the socio-cultural setting where the message was revealed. Making Muhammad precede the Qur'an is significant: the messenger comes before the message: were it not for the former, the latter would not exist. We shall subsequently see that the Prophet is not, in Charfi's eyes, a passive instrument, he is active in revelation and in its shaping. The Qur'an and the message flow from the phenomenon of the Prophet and his personality. In spite of the paucity of sources in the chronicles about the status of Muhammad before his prophetic mission and even afterwards in Mecca, Abdelmajid Charfi deduces that he was not an important personality in Meccan society or among his own people, despite the claims of biographical literature. He was an ordinary man integrated into the culture of his *milieu*, sharing in its mentality and belonging to his milieu in the usual ways. Abdelmajid Charfi does not deny that Muhammad practised the religion of his people before the beginning of his mission. It seems to us that this observation is correct in the light of marginal reports that Muhammad was fervent in his religious practice, otherwise the question of the ritual assembly on 'Arafāt would not have been significant. Traditional accounts also mention his piety, a spiritual and devout attitude which could be linked to the pious figures of the pre-Islamic period and to the pious persons living in proximity to the Kaaba; thereby discarding subsequent Islamic interpretations in order to recover the meaning of the term "piety" in pre-Islamic Arabia. The same is true of accounts of the Prophet eating according to pagan liturgical usages, according to the names of the idols he pronounced. Ibn al Kalbi mentions in the *Book of Idols* the question of 'Uzza: "I sacrificed to 'Uzza a dust-coloured ewe while I was a follower of the religion of my people."[5] There is nothing here to cast shame on Muhammad as he had not yet assumed his prophetic mission. On the contrary these are credible links between Muhammad and his milieu and culture.

The Prophecy of Muhammad: a Composite Prophecy

Biographers stressed that Muhammad was chosen for his mission on grounds of merit. A contrary point of view would sometimes emerge between schools of Muslim thought in subsequent theological debates about the question of prophecy: was he chosen on grounds of merit or, rather, preferment? Charfi has reoriented the question toward an examination of the historical and social context, to uncover the question of preparedness for prophecy and the truthfulness of Muhammad in what he contemplated and subsequently expressed initially to a small group of friends, before proclaiming his message to the crowd in the sacred precinct. Charfi's opinion is that Muhammad was aware of other religions because of his journeys and his contact, either by chance or on purpose, with men of religion and others. This was not unconventional for his time. Muhammad was seeking piety. He was devoted to his spiritual quest. He was also in contact with spiritual figures. As a result of his meditation he was certain that God had chosen him to proclaim the message (*Islam: Between Message and History*, p. 40). Charfi does not exclude the possibility that the prophecy of Muhammad may have been a composite prophecy joining together previous prophecies among the people of Israel and in the Arabian peninsula (*Islam: Between Message and History*, p. 45), embracing preceding prophecies save elements which had been abrogated (*Islam: Between Message and History*, p. 43).

This reliance on preceding prophets was important in order to "steady" the Prophet, as in Sūra 20:99 of the Qur'an: "And We relate to you all the accounts of Noble Messengers, in order to steady your heart with it." The significance of Muhammad emerges in this compilation of previous prophecies and their arrangement in a manner suited to the people of his time, their mentality and their preoccupations without, however, blending with their own points of view or their religious or moral opinions. Had he done this he would not have been a prophet nor would he have faced violent opposition (*Islam: Between Message and History*, p. 46). Muhammad was genuine in his prophecy and in his sharing with the people of his time, his experience of God in a profound and moving way. He had perceived the absolute and contemplated infinity and the invisible.

He was deeply convinced of the authenticity of these experiences (*Islam: Between Message and History*, p. 42). He communicated this experience in a cultural form expressing a new way of perceiving the world while dispelling some of the existential anxiety people experienced. Muhammad was not, therefore, a passive prophet (*Islam: Between Message and History*, p. 44); he was determined and able to influence others. He did not, however, perform miracles, contrary to prevailing Muslim belief and scholarly evidence. The claim that the Qur'an was a miracle of Muhammad's was a claim invented by scholars in the same way that they invented miracles and attributed them to him. They interiorised all these inventions which then became the object of veneration.

Muhammad as the Seal of Prophecy

It has become a widespread belief among Muslims that the question of the seal of prophecy is a clear and unambiguous matter: Muhammad is the last of the prophets and there is none after him. Many thinkers considered that Islam represented the highest form of maturity and evolution among the messages of the three monotheist religions.

Two other opinions developed which helped to open up a new horizon of meaning: the Baha'i interpretation is the first of these. The Baha'i understanding was that the Prophet Muhammad did not close the door of revelation necessary to sustain religion, nor was he the last of the prophets; but rather that religion is completed and enhanced by him. This means that Muhammad is among the prophets the one who confers upon them honour and distinction, while the messages of God to his servants are continuous and eternal.[6] The second opinion is that of Muhammad Iqbal, who thought that prophecy when it was completed carried within itself the element leading to its disappearance. This means that human responsibility begins when prophecy is interrupted and ended.

Abdelmadjid Charfi was aware of the opinion common among Muslims and of these other two points of view. He introduced an original way of looking at the question of the seal of prophecy. The seal of prophecy, according to Charfi, can be likened to someone closing the door of his house from the interior, remaining a prisoner of the house. It can also be compared with someone closing the door from the outside and who benefits from the contents of the house and what is outside. The opinion deeply rooted among Muslim scholars and many hadith scholars is that Muhammad closed the preceding prophetic messages from the interior of the house; he is the last of the Prophets and there is no life for the believer save within this enclosed environment. This view of prophecy is a constricting one, contradicting the historical law of alternation and change. For that reason Charfi believes that the closure was a closure from the outside, putting an end definitively to the need for people to rely on resources other than their own. The task of the Prophet of Islam is, therefore, to guide people to a new sense of responsibility and to accept the results of their own choices (*Islam: Between Message and History*, p. 80).

Many of these insights seem far removed from the logic of the stories in traditional sources which have influenced the orientations of religious and cultural practice. In terms of contemporary Islamic thought they are original interpretations of the heritage of the past, including perceptions of the person of Muhammad. The Muhammad present in the writings of Charfi is different from the magical representation of Muhammad inherited from the past. He has managed to connect Muhammad, prophet and person, with the prevailing mentality in his society and culture. Prophecy, therefore, was a visible phenomenon, and in the conscience of the Prophet, an appropriate source of knowledge to which all previous prophecies contributed. Muhammad was confirmed in his mission by this knowledge, and genuine in his proclamation of it. Charfi's point of view is important in that it reconsidered attitudes interiorised by Muslims and written down by scholars; on grounds of their venerable history these attitudes have become part of cultural and religious practice, considered by the majority of Muslims to be the gauge of their piety, even if they were contrary to the Qur'an.

The Phenomenon of the Qur'an

Discussions of the phenomenon of the Qur'an entail research about the kind of culture amid which the Qur'an appeared, within which it interacted and from which it derived its linguistic means of expression and its instruments of discourse. It also supposes an examination of the mission of the Prophet as a whole, its social origins, the horizons of its thought, its existential preoccupations and the ways of receiving the revelation communicated by the Prophet. This leads in turn to the history of the Qur'an and how it took form. Abdelmadjid Charfi, with his keen anthropological sense, was aware of all these questions in his examination of the culture and the mentality which the discourse of the Qur'an penetrated and which the message shaped, thus acquiring its basic characteristics.

The first of these characteristics is that the culture in which Qur'anic discourse took form was an oral culture. This is essential when deciding on the meaning of a verse sent down as revelation to the Prophet as the person being addressed does not know who is addressing him. Understanding the original meaning of a verse is, therefore, difficult. If one adds the question of the growth of revelatory discourse over twenty-two years, one may realise the difficulty confronting those who claim that they possess the original meaning of the Qur'an. Further complications arise when the researcher realises that it is impossible to recover the oral context of revelation and the situation of those hearing the revelation. In order to get round this difficulty, Muslims, scholars and simple believers alike have believed that the book composed between two covers is the Qur'an. This is a mere hypothesis grounded in popular devotion.

The second characteristic of the message of the Qur'an is that the people to whom it was addressed had a mentality heavily influenced by a sense of the sacred and by myth (*Islam: Between Message and History*, p. 46). It is, therefore, natural that Qur'anic discourse should reflect this way of thinking, with its miscellaneous images, examples, parables and stories, to say nothing of the rhythm of the discourse and the mysterious letters which scholars did not understand despite their voluminous writings on the subject. All these elements form a mythical horizon for the discourse of the Qur'an, one that is appropriate to the mentality of the Arabs of the peninsula who received the text. Yet behind these stylistic features, the person receiving the revelation is the one concerned by the message. For the message to have a meaning among its followers and in human history, the content of the message has to change with the mentalities of the times. Otherwise the text remains silent and inanimate. The solution that Charfi approves is to disregard the circumstantial commands and interdictions necessary at the time of the revelation (even if it was of fundamental importance) and to present the latent aims and intentions.

This second characteristic (the influence of myth) had a decisive effect on legislation. Charfi has voiced audacious opinions on legislation connected with liturgy and social relations. He states that the revelation never alludes to Sharīʿa in terms of divine law, but uses it to mean a way, one of the meanings of the term "Sharīʿa" (*Islam: Between Message and History*, p. 59). This is the general meaning and the profound vision delimitated by the aims of the message. The judgments in the Qur'an are few in number and varied in content, so it is more accurate to consider them as general pedagogical and moral orientations (*Islam: Between Message and History*, p. 60). The few details of judgments that Muslims may find in the Qur'an are circumstantial in character and cannot be set down definitively for all time. A literal approach to the text and the few judgments therein is a sort of veneration of the letter of the text, removed from its historical context and from the mentality of the person receiving the text. Those who treat the text in this arbitrary way, neglect the higher aims of the text and cling instead to a particular set of transient historical circumstances whose protagonists have passed away.

The Qur'an did not give detailed instructions about liturgy and prayer, but merely gave impressionistic suggestions of a type suitable to a mentality influenced by myth and legend. It is strange that scholars invented artifices and stories to support the putting in place of detailed instructions about religious observances. Prayer, alms-giving, the pilgrimage, fasting, even jihād, sometimes included in the pillars of Islam; their aim is the service of God or social solidarity or an expression of faith in the one God, as in the pilgrimage for example. Ritual and ceremony are mere forms; the decisive point is the spiritual aim behind them, or the reforming, moral or educational intention. These can be validly achieved without the outward cultic forms.

The *Sunna*'s insistence on word-for-word details of religious usage and practice did not take into account the mentality of the society in which the revelation took place. Such an approach is concerned with the form, not the aims, of the message. The same is true of relations between people as the Qur'an did not give detailed judgments in a number of important matters such as apostasy, the system of government, family organisation and economic questions in general. There are general succinct allusions to stealing and adultery, although these are general allusions taking account of prevailing mentalities with regard to social relations. These stipulations are determined by their historical circumstances and the prevailing mentality of society. They are not decisive; the educational and moral aim of the message expressed through such stipulations is of primary importance. The aim of the message is pedagogical and moral; it is not an instrument of legislation by means of a few summary provisions. The message of the Qur'an aims at attaining religious freedom, preventing slavery, securing equality between men and women and the elimination of abuse in all its forms. Attention should be given to these values when endeavouring to understand the discourse of the Qur'an as well as popular piety. The Prophet's life needs to be considered in the same way; deeds of his which are considered exemplary and binding are only expressions of the mission he assumed with his Companions: one that entailed changing mentalities and behaviour inconsistent with the message of the Qur'an (see *Islam: Between Message and History*, p. 68). The reader may be surprised by examples of killing, violence and slavery perpetrated by followers of the Prophet or with his knowledge, although these were prevailing practices that necessarily disappeared with the passage of time.

These opinions seem striking and audacious. Charfi's far-reaching conclusions are based on the theory of the aims and the intentions of the Qur'an. He did not invent this theory, although those who developed it did not go as far as Charfi in his elaboration of it, neither Shatibi, nor al-Shawkani nor Allal al Fasi or Ben Achour, for example. Charfi has applied a point of view which is seen today as his most important and original contribution to the renewal of Islamic thought; that is, his understanding of the notion of the seal of prophecy as a description of the message of the Prophet. The aims of the message of Muhammad can, therefore, be seen as a seal of prophecy applied from the outside, contrary to the representations produced by scholars in Islamic history.

Islam in History: Closure from the Interior?

Charfi states unhesitatingly that successive generations of Muslims were not faithful to the intentions of the Qur'an and that they sometimes deviated from it due to attitudes lacking in refinement. He seeks a justification for this point of view through the study of three phases which saw the development of attitudes which departed from the intentions of the Qur'an: the succession to the Prophet; the formation of the religious establishment; and the theoretical reflection accompanying it. Regarding the succession, were the Muslim community faithful to spiritual and religious values when choosing Abu Bakr? Charfi's reply is clearly negative.

It was the favoured solution, one that imposed itself due to the weakness of other solutions. The succession could have taken place on a tribal basis, as was the case before the time of Muhammad, although the changes introduced by the message of the Prophet made this impossible. A second solution was for wealthy members of the Quraysh tribe to take control: this also proved impossible. It was thought that a third solution was possible: succession according to the *Sahīfa* or "Constitution of Medina", a procedure that had not yet finally taken established, institutional form. Harbingers of a fourth "solution" appeared: a civil war over the succession, although prospects of such a turn of events quickly receded. At the *Saqīfa* (the term used for negotiations preceding the designation of Abū Bakr), signs of possible conflict emerged again. A fifth possibility would have been for power to have been entrusted to the people of the House, the close relatives of the prophet such as 'Alī or al 'Abbās. Opposition, notably to 'Alī, and the weakness of his supporters at that time eliminated this possibility. Finally, Abū Bakr was designated as successor: he was the oldest, most experienced and had personal charisma. He was also, according to traditional accounts, a genealogist. Religious considerations did not come into consideration in Abū Bakr's designation. The question seems not to have concerned the Muslim community as much as it did those wielding power and influence. This is contrary to the spirit of equality between Muslims (*Islam: Between Message and History*, p. 92). The same can be said of the enslavement of captives during the conquest, and is even clearer with regard to excessive tax collection and the treatment of women, all accepted by the collective Muslim conscience and firmly rooted in culture and law. Perceived today as part of a Muslim golden age, they are contrary to the higher aims of the message: a call to freedom, social concord, helping the weak, equality between the sexes and protection of human dignity. The entrenchment of these attitudes and practices contrary to the spirit of the higher aims of the message was due to their taking on an institutional form: this is what Charfi terms "institutionalisation". In his view there were three phases in this process: distinguishing between Muslims and non-Muslims in complete contradiction to the message of the Prophet which called for mutual knowledge and cooperation in order to develop understanding between peoples. A study of the edicts relating to the *Dhimmis* reveal a series of punitive measures which marginalise minorities, in contradiction to the message of Islam and the most basic human values.

The second process involved the codification of prayer and religious practices without any real reflection; religious practice became form and ritual, whereas previously meditation on the message was intended to attain the moral and pedagogical aim of the message.

The third process turned religion into an institution by codifying the way (whereas in reality there is more than one way) to believe, contrary to the message of Muhammad, with its broad acceptance of various ways of believing and its aim of bringing people together around common spiritual values in the cause of peace and progress. The theoretical basis of the institution was laid down by scholars in the following areas: jurisprudence and its origins; exegesis; hadīth; theology; and Sufism. The most important deduction by Abdelmadjid Charfi in the field of jurisprudence (*fiqh*) is that rites and prayer were laid down in detail on a non-Qur'anic basis, so disconnecting ritual from its spiritual aims. Conduct unconnected with Islam was sanctified by scholars on the grounds that it was an imitation of the ancestors. Charfi also deduces that scholars progressively created a barrier preventing Muslims from directly encountering the Qur'an, a tendency that manifested itself in the way that culturally influenced *sunna* isolated believers from the sacred text (*Islam: Between Message and History*, p. 126).

The same was true of the study of the origins of jurisprudence; the theory created by Shāfiʿī detailed the ways of dealing with Prophetic discourse, preventing even the basic freedom that Muslims would have enjoyed, were it not for the decision of Shāfiʿī, author of the *Risāla*, that no judgment was to be made without proof in the Book of God. Thus, the interpretative effort to ascertain the aims of the message of the Prophet and the responsibility of the individual were reduced to making analogical judgments based on a preceding case. In every case legal scholars wanted to surround judgments with a dense hedge of definitive prescriptions taking no account of changing circumstances which modified systems and the content of legislation.

Qur'anic commentary was not exempt from this tendency to hedge the text with prescriptive commentary. It is clear in this field of Muslim erudition that scholars prescribed in detail the ways of dealing with the Qur'anic text. They rarely examined the real difficulties arising from the language of the Qur'an, the link between verses and the question of abrogation; or speculation about the circumstances of revelation. Culture and traditional practice prevented any personal effort outside the limits laid down. As pointed out in *Islam: Between Message and History* the interpretation defended by a particular school of thought was even more rigid.

Hadīth is another example of how scholars deviated from the aims of the Qur'an. Contrary to the Prophet's wishes, hadīth were codified. Hadīth were surrounded with an aura of sanctity and Shāfi'ī went so far as to say that the wisdom mentioned in Sūra 4:138 "God has sent down to you the scripture and wisdom" is the Sunna. Falsification of hadīth, as each sect sought to legitimise its authority and marginalise its rivals, use of hadīth as a commentary on religious practice and ever more detailed judgments and directives for prayer and worship: these are the real dilemmas for the freedom and conscience of Muslims. Hadīth collections must be subjected to rigorous critical examination. The Turkish Department of Religious affairs announced in February 2008 a plan to revise the hadīth collections and remove elements contrary to the original intentions of the message and its humanistic values.

Charfi's revision of how theology and Sufism are understood is similarly radical. Theologians and compilers of manuals of belief all belonged to a particular sect and stipulated in detail what belief entailed, in their opinion. They prevented free speculation and deviation (considered as unbelief) from their views. As a result they legitimised the division of the community, while claiming to speak for a religion whose original aspiration was to create a single, united entity, bound together by resilient solidarity, equality and creativity derived from the diversity of its origins and resources.

From this historico-critical analysis and a close reading of various sources representative of Islamic disciplines Charfi deduces that Muslim scholars were not faithful to the aims of the message of Muhammad, which was intended as an "open" conclusion to previous prophetic messages. It drew inspiration from the accumulated messages of the past, and gave Muslims their due part of responsible freedom in order that they might create according to their desires, on the condition that they accept the consequences of their creativity.

Charfi has "unpacked" the religious establishment, exposing its functioning. He has exposed in detail how Muslim scholars have sacrificed the aims of the message and practice of the Prophet, and its humanistic values. In so doing Charfi calls for a departure from the confines of codified institutionalisation and a move toward freedom and creativity, in keeping with the aims of the message of the Prophet. The true Muslim in his eyes is one who is innovative and creative, not one who follows in the footsteps of the ancestors, valid though their experience may have been. Charfi sees true religion as giving meaning to human life in the context of the cosmos, its origins and ultimate destiny. Humankind thus rises above the animal level to that of the free, responsible, thinking person. In Charfi's words: "the human person worthy of the name is not intellectually lazy, but confronts his existential and relational difficulties in a responsible manner."[7]

A Call for a Free and Responsible Muslim Conscience

The solution that Charfi proposes is for today's Muslims to understand and reflect upon the aims and exigencies of the message of Muhammad. They should also shake off the authority of the religious establishment and of culturally determined religious practice. This means in practice that Muslims should embrace secularism, an important consequence of modernity in contemporary society. Secular Muslims are aware of historico-critical practices and realise that religion is not synonymous with the religious establishment. They are also aware that subservience to ancestral practice restricts individual freedom and destroys moral responsibility. They realise that the domination of minor details constricts believers with codes and rules and narrows down the spiritual horizon of the message, a horizon that believers shape for themselves.

One of the least attractive images of Muslims today is that of people somehow split down the middle, who belong neither to the past (in terms of its preoccupations and ways of thinking), nor to the present with its challenges and rapid changes in the field of technology and learning. Charfi sees the only solution as being a resolute choice in favour of the present instead of the past and the exercise of free personal judgment rather than deferring to others. Free thought and assumption of the consequences of one's decisions are the basis for the moral dimension of the Muslim conscience. Muslims today can interiorise Qur'anic morality not according to the schemas of past luminaries, but by concentrating on the universal values toward which the message of the Prophet was directed, going beyond solutions linked to particular circumstances, values that define the characteristics of fully human individuals worthy of the position their Creator has entrusted to them.

This informed conscience understands the wide-ranging nature of the call for the application of the Shari'a today and realises that the inheritance of men and women must be equal, applying the principle of authority between sexes. Such a conscience also understands that legislating for civil institutions on the basis of religion and dogma is an incorrect way of proceeding which undermines the organisation of society, setting people against one another on account of illusory symbols. This accompanies an awareness that morality among Muslims today is not defined in terms of rites and liturgies and Qur'anic commands and interdictions; rather morality defines the values of freedom, responsibility, equality and solidarity, justice and mutual respect which together realise human happiness. These are the aims of the message of Muhammad, as well as the forms and means which guarantee the application of these values today. Thus, the modern Muslim conscience is faithful to the aims of the Prophet's message and the values of modernity. The Muslim is not a stranger to the period in which he or she is living.

This invitation issued by Abdelmadjid Charfi is based on serious research and a significant intellectual venture embarked upon by a scholar from a Muslim society. It is serious because it runs counter to the current which seeks to entrench the power of culturally determined religious practice, an adventure because its outcome cannot be guaranteed among Muslims themselves. Rigorous research, adherence to the principle of unfettered thought, moral responsibility and intellectual integrity: in the case of Abdelmadjid Charfi these mean a putting into practice the aims of the message of Islam and the exercise of individual discernment (*ijitihād*) in a non-fundamentalist way.

The reader may wonder how to categorise this book and its author: is it a piece of academic research carried out by a university teacher competent in his domain and able to organise the methods and basis for his work in a Tunisian university setting? Or is it an intellectual enterprise where an author has endeavoured to follow a particular theory and provoke the curiosity of Muslims, traditionally protected against uncertainty and questioning by a parrot-like repetition of tradition, without finding therein anything of help to them today, or any spiritual sustenance capable of responding to their present aspirations? Or is it a literary work in the traditional sense of the term, rebelling against false values and revealing authentic values which enable the life of the mind to rediscover its mission of enlightenment? Do the book and its author thus represent a new voice of reform? Let the reader make what he or she wills of the book. It is indisputably a book which challenges and unsettles its readers, preventing them from following obediently where others lead them. In this book resonates an echo, one hitherto hidden by a mere illusion of truth which has enveloped readers from a Muslim background, no longer able to make up their own minds. Readers from other backgrounds will find in this book elements that they do not hear amid the prevailing false and vacuous hubbub of voices. They will be surprised that the book does not conform to the usual patterns. They will find precise analysis, truth, audacious interpretation, examples quoted from cultures and learning of varied origins, as well as from a variety of philosophical schools. They will wonder how these various elements are forged into a captivating whole.

The book had an impact in the Arab world as well as in Iran, while scholars and commentators in France appreciated the book prior to its translation into English. There was general agreement that the book's publication was an "event". They perhaps meant by that that they found a novel type of intellectual rigour from within the Muslim community. In the case of Charfi the human sciences have enriched an original point of view, one where concepts are clear, where opinions are not forced or manipulated and whose structure is sound. Here, then, is a book which may enrich what readers already possess in the way of culture and intellectual resources. We wish success both to the book and to its readers.

Part One

*Characteristics of the Message
of Muhammad*

1
History and Theory

D
efining a prophetic message in a general sense is relatively easy; it can be described as the discourse that a prophet communicates to his contemporaries, his community and to people in general. However, the interpretations of prophecy and its content are many and varied. Prophecy and inspiration are among the most difficult terms to deal with, as their meaning changes over time, along with religions and cultures. These terms are also connected with the term "God", "that mystery which divides us even as it reveals itself and binds us together when it inhabits us".[1]

The task of defining the term "prophetic message" is rendered more difficult by the fact that it evokes unique historical experiences which cannot be relived at second-hand. The protagonists involved were human, although they were invested with qualities uncommon among ordinary people; qualities which attracted followers and disciples who believed in their message and strove to spread it. They believed in a spontaneous way, and they did not theorise the content of their belief until some time after the proclamation of the prophetic message. As far as the history of Islamic thought is concerned, this theorising took place only in the context of *'ilm al kalām* (theology); it was not an initial concern of the community, more occupied with the political situation than with the rational organisation of the tenets of belief and their content.

For the moment, therefore, the contribution of the theologians has been left aside, in order to re-examine what the history of religions has to say about prophecy and inspiration. Thereafter, close reading of the text of the Qur'an will take us beyond the dense layers of interpretation (which hide as much as they reveal) to uncover the historical reality behind the text. This means reexamining the tales of the *Sīra* (biography of the Prophet), although we know that they were compiled only after the events that they narrate and that they are a "reading" of history which reflects the writer's own situation (Ibn Sa'ad, Ibn Ishāq, Ibn Hishām, Tabari), as well as the events that befell the Muslim community after the death of the Prophet, notably during the period between the death of the Prophet and the compilation of his biography. In other words, they are a particular representation of the events of the Prophet's life, a representation influenced by external circumstances, ambiguous to some extent, and so to be treated with caution. It is clear that a communal folk-memory does not record exactly the events of a hero's life, but transforms him into a kind of archetype invested with the qualities required by his mission. It does not soberly record historical events but presents them in a way that reflects the ideal qualities of the heroic founder figure.

Manifestations of the sacred and forms of religious practice and profession have varied widely throughout history, as excavations and successive archaeological discoveries have shown. Traditional religions, mysticism and prophetic revelations provide further examples of this diversity. Not all the characteristics of traditional beliefs will be examined at this point, since their variety makes it difficult to present them in a summary fashion without the risk of deformation: these include, among many other examples, ritual celebrations of the yearly cycle of seasons organised in agricultural societies at the beginning and end of the planting season, rites connected with death and significant events in the life cycle such as birth, puberty, marriage and illness, the conferral of a sacred status to trees and places, the sanctification of natural phenomena such as the sun and certain planets, the veneration of idols, the deification of rulers and the myths which narrate the lives of heroes and gods. We are essentially concerned with the stages through which humankind passed in its search for the meaning of existence, explaining the origin and destiny of human life and creating a belief system as a bulwark against the apparent disorder of creation.

Human existence requires a structured environment of some kind, which entails giving a specific order and coherence to events and phenomena, be they part of the natural world or arising within human society. Understanding and accounting for such phenomena provides a defence against the vagaries of blind chance or hazard. Once such a *Weltanschauung* has been elaborated, it undergoes continual refinement, thus creating culture, with its material and spiritual dimensions. Culture is one of humankind's particular attributes, which distinguishes it from animals. The instruments, institutions and values which together create culture acquire, with the passage of time, a certain autonomy and cohesion. These are then considered part of the very nature of things, and once "interiorised", to use the sociological term, humans obey these institutions and values automatically, forgetting that they are, in reality, human creations.[2] Human creativity, in any field, engenders a subsequent series of creations which acquire autonomy and objectivity, and are continually "interiorised" in a dialectic fashion. In other words, in early history humankind languished in a state of alienation, unaware of the meaning of its actions and of what constituted authentically human behaviour at a personal or collective level.

Simply as an example, one can observe that societies lay down rules and constraints to govern sexual relations. Such rules vary from one society to another, but they are nonetheless present, defining what is permissible and licit, or forbidden and illicit. These rules are integrated into the structure of the individual's personality. Self-knowledge is thus acquired by interiorising the ways in which society considers the individual. A successful education and upbringing means that social rules will seem evident to the individual and he or she will not transgress them, or imagine that he or she might transgress them, without feeling guilt and remorse. If a person does not follow these rules and is sanctioned for that, he or she will consider him or herself guilty and deserving of punishment. Other forms of relations within society function in the same way. Through a comprehensive observance of the laws prevailing within society, the individual is brought to accept the status quo, without any inclination to rebel against the established order of things or to transgress it. No alternative to what is already familiar and allows the group to function can be contemplated by the individual. People will even willingly sacrifice themselves so that these values may be respected when their tribe, people, or nation is engaged in conflict.

Religion has historically played a fundamental part in conferring absolute legitimacy on options taken at a particular time. Social institutions thus receive a validity which goes beyond their historical reality, anchoring them in a common origin surrounded by a halo of sanctity. These institutions thus appear as though they are a reflection of the cosmos itself. This latter is a continuous circular movement manifesting itself in successive natural phenomena which triumph over chaos, a movement which humans reenact symbolically through liturgy and its concomitant expressions and gestures. The most ancient forms of religiosity are characterised, *inter alia*, by the belief that transient human actions are inscribed in an order of continuity and permanence, invested with quasi-divine attributes. Individuals and societies can thus face up to their own mortality as it is believed to be part of a sacred temporal continuum.

Religion's role of legitimisation, an integral part of all religions, took on an animist form in primitive religions which imagined a world in which human-kind was not distinct from other elements of the created order. These religions were based on a number of founding myths which explain the nature of existence in general and were characterised by a belief in magic, particularly with regard to words pronounced by individuals considered capable of directing the course of events. Ritual played a highly important role in maintaining the equilibrium of existence and in integrating the individual into society.[3]

It is in this context that the phenomenon of offering sacrifices to remote, mysterious deities can be observed. Sacrifices, sometimes entailing human offerings (the eldest son, an unmarried daughter), or more generally involving specific animals, are not intended only to placate the gods or ask for fertility, but also to restore an equilibrium that has been lost. This was necessary in cases of drought, floods, tornadoes and earthquakes, or when a society's laws and usages had been transgressed. Those officiating in these rites, which included sacrifices, were aware of their magical and religious significance and hoped that through these rites the continued stability of existence would be guaranteed. The healthy development of animals, abundant prey for hunters, as well as harvests and fruitful trees, the birth of children without any defects, the regular succession of the hours and the seasons, all of this depended on carrying out certain rituals. If this order of things was disturbed in any way, humans considered themselves responsible for this and the prescribed rites had to be carried out in order to return events to their normal course.

This form of religious practice continued in various forms throughout the prehistoric era, in particular before the invention of writing and the growth of more developed and complex forms of religious practice. Indian and Asian religions will not be examined in any detail, as their influence on the monotheist religions of the Near East was a limited one. It is worth observing, however, that traditional religions left a residual deposit, as it were, in the monotheist belief systems. This is particularly clear in the Judaeo-Christian Bible. Among these are, for example, the magic effect of words pronounced in particular circum-stances, and the ancient belief that plants and animals attained full existence only when they received a name. Another example is the notion that human-kind was created from clay; traces of this exist in Sumerian beliefs. The story of Creation in the Old Testament contains a number of elements belonging to ancient religions: the existence of an imaginary land between two rivers is clearly of Babylonian origin; the episode in which Adam eats the fruit of the tree and loses his immortality echoes the story of Gilgamesh who also loses his immor-tality. As for the sacrifices mentioned in the Bible, it is one of the elements of Canaanite ritual in which offerings are considered food for the gods, although it is also present in ancient religions and among many peoples and cultures. A standing stone could also be a symbol of divine presence and this belief was current among the inhabitants of the Arabian Peninsula even before Biblical times. Sacrifices were offered in proximity to the stone, particularly at the begin-ning of spring. Other symbols and rites which existed in the region were also retained in Biblical times, although they were invested with new significance.

Belief in the one God may well represent a new element introduced by Judaism, although the Torah does not so much deny the existence of other gods as insist that the God of Moses does not brook the acceptance of other rival gods. Baal was the god of the Canaanites and among the Hebrews his cult was associated with that of "El" and "Yahweh", finally becoming one single deity. The final separation, and rejection of the cult of Baal, took place only in the seventh or eighth century BCE. It is also noteworthy that the Torah presents a God who is human in his qualities and weaknesses: he is capable of love and hate, happi-ness and sadness, he pardons, he exacts revenge, and so on. However, he does not have the failings of the Greek gods; in particular, he does not tolerate mockery.

The survival of certain elements of traditional belief systems should not, however, lead the observer to neglect the radical novelty of monotheist religion and the rupture it provoked with traditional systems. Even the resemblance between God and man is only one of God's attributes: the other is that of a radical otherness, a sole Being, surrounded by heavenly creatures. He is the absolute judge, representing a desire for perfection and purity in an absolute form. It is not surprising that monotheist religions do not contain traces of the conflict between heavenly forces present in many other religions, and that monotheism's proponents across the centuries contain a proportion of fanatics, in the light of their desire to assume divine qualities. At the same time, they attach importance (in a way that Hindu deities do not) to the principles and the practice of morality, and historical events possess a religious significance insofar as they are manifestations of the divinity. Another example of this would be the interdiction to consume the fruit of the tree in the Garden of Paradise: a new idea took form here, unrelated to the symbolism traditionally associated with the tree, namely the significance of knowledge as something possessing existential value, together with the fact that science has the power to transform the foundations of human existence.[4]

At the heart of the radical novelty of monotheism was its advocacy of human responsibility for all actions, especially those considered evil. God, on the other hand, was held to be innocent of all involvement. God addresses man for the first time in the Old Testament when he addresses Abraham, asking him to do certain things and promising others. God, however, is not affected by the nature of the subsequent actions of Abraham, nor does he "need" them in any way. Human refractoriness does not lead, as was the case before, to some kind of instability in the natural order. The bond between Abraham and his God is one of faith. Those who offered sacrifices were aware of their value, as we noted earlier, whereas Abraham did not understand the meaning of the sacrifice of his son when this was requested of him. He responds to the call of faith alone when he is on the point of sacrificing his son. It is this faith which sustains Abraham and sustains humankind as a whole in the face of difficulties, trials and experiences throughout life. The figure of Job, together with that of Abraham, embodies this deep faith which does not waver despite the severe trials of the believer.

Even if the historians of religion are inclined for the most part to deny the notion of a linear evolution from polytheism to monotheism, insisting, on the contrary, on the permanence of certain common elements in religious experiences of different kinds, that does not deny the quantitative leap represented by monotheism within the history of religions. It reduced the role of magic within religion and considered events within their historical context. It gave importance to a system of belief in which reason played a part. The notion of prophecy, too, underwent notable changes. Making prophecies while in a state of trance was a phenomenon which existed in Canaanite religion, and around 1000 BCE the Hebrews encountered prophets in Palestine while at the same time having their own seers during their period as nomads. Subsequently, the term of prophet and that of seer came to be synonymous. The prophets were of two kinds: those who were affiliated to cultic institutions, joining the priests in the celebration of their liturgies. Certain of these prophets were accused of being charlatans. A second category uttered prophecies not in their capacity as functionaries of the temple cult, but because God had chosen them as prophets. This gave them the power to foretell the future and transcend the laws of nature. When they prophesied, they fell prey to strange afflictions including paralysis, fainting, stupors and rolling on the ground. They were convinced, in particular, that they were not speaking of their own accord, but were communicating the word of God, together with his orders and prescriptions. The Old Testament has immortalised the prophecies of Isaiah, Jeremiah, Ezekiel and Amos, who lived between the eighth and the fifth centuries BCE. Abraham, Lot, Isaac and Jacob were considered patriarchs rather than prophets. Prophecy, in the sense of the communication of a divine message, was a Jewish phenomenon, which explains the opposition to the prophecies of Muhammad when he appeared among the *Ummiyin* (a term which means "non-Jewish", rather than "illiterate" as many commentators have imagined).[5]

When Jesus initiated his preaching in Palestine, his contemporaries, whether they had adhered to his teaching or not, interpreted his message in the light of contemporary Jewish representations of prophecy. The occupation that a Messiah would save his people from the yoke of foreign expectation also influenced popular reactions to Jesus' teaching, together with what were taken to be signs of the imminent end of the world and the coming of an age of harmony when the wolf would go out to pasture with the lamb without doing it any harm. Doctrines concerning such subjects as the relationship between Jesus and God, the incarnation in the person of Jesus, the Word or "Logos" and the understanding of sacrifice were all developed by the first generations of Christians after the Church seceded from the Jewish community, due to the influence of Paul in particular. The spread of Christianity among Gentile nations influenced by Hellenic and various Gnostic currents of thought also contributed to this process of doctrinal elaboration.[6]

The Arabian Peninsula, and in particular the region of Hejaz, was not isolated from the various religious and cultural currents existing throughout the Near East, whether in Syria, Palestine, Egypt, or Mesopotamia, and the neighbouring Persian empire. Geopolitical boundaries, in the modern sense of the word, did not exist between the various centres of population separating them from one another. Various forms of commercial contact, together with conflict and crises such as famines, meant that cross-cultural exchanges took place in an ongoing and reciprocal fashion. The pilgrimage to Mecca and markets were occasions during which different currents of thought and belief converged. The birth of Islam in the early seventh century CE should be seen not only as a natural prolongation of the Judaeo-Christian monotheism present in the region, but also as part of the religious evolution of humankind across the centuries. This does not mean that the prevailing conditions in Mecca and the surrounding region should be neglected, but they should not, on the other hand, be considered as the sole determining influence on the message of Muhammad, as though this were simply a reaction to these conditions or a reworking of the pre-Islamic heritage. Much of Western scholarship concerning the early development of Islam is marked by this approach, which, despite appearances, is influenced by ideas which circulated in medieval Europe about Islam.[7] The message of Muhammad presented itself as a continuation of previous religious teaching, and there is no reason why it should not be accepted in this light, especially as this interpretation is confirmed by objective historical analysis.

While monotheism may have initially developed in a Jewish environment, it was permeated by anthropomorphism as well as by residual traces of the religions that had preceded it.[8] For example, the notion that God had spoken on occasion under the collective name "Elohim", and that he was the God of a particular people rather than a kind of cosmic God. Rituals and prohibitions occupied an important place in the Old Testament, and early Judaism had no conception of the resurrection and everlasting life after death.[9] Christianity, with the doctrines of the Trinity, the Incarnation, the special status of Mary and the saints and their relics, led to a drift away from a pure form of monotheism to a greater or lesser extent. It is certain that the Jewish and Christian communities existing in the regions of Hejaz or the north and south of the Arabian Peninsula were not, religiously speaking, of a high level of refinement, nor did they participate (with the exception of the community of Hira) in any meaningful way in the theological development which Egypt and Syria experienced. A Bedouin, oral character marked popular culture in the Jewish and Christian communities and led to a blend between their respective cultures and local elements of popular belief. A distance opened up between these forms of religious faith and official doctrine as elaborated by rabbis and theologians, who had attained a high level in theological reflection and the study of the textual sources on which doctrine was based.

The Hejaz, cradle of Islam, was ready at the beginning of the seventh century CE to receive the new religion. The foundations of tribal society had begun to weaken due to the rise of Mecca as a position of power and influence and organisation, which made it a hub of religious and economic activity throughout the whole Arabian Peninsula. The ongoing wars between the Persian and Byzantine empires, together with the weakness of Yemen in the face of their competition, played an important role in modifying the existing trade routes between Asia, Europe and Africa, placing them under the control of the Quraysh. Qurayshi merchants, moreover, had succeeded through a system of alliances in guaranteeing the security of caravans. They were able to ensure that a share of the profits went to tribes through whose territory the caravans passed.[10] This situation gave rise to a kind of tacit recognition of the Quraysh's preeminence, as revenue generated by trade was added to the symbolic authority derived from the pilgrimage to the Kaaba, in addition to the Quraysh's control of the system of protection and assistance granted to pilgrims. They also organised Meccan life through an incipient institutional structure consisting of an assembly of notables from each clan (*batnun*) which met in the *Dar en Nadwa* to discuss community affairs and determine norms for individual conduct.

These changes affecting social organisation in the Arabian Peninsula as a whole, and especially Hejaz from the sixth century CE onward, were destined to have a profound effect on the way in which religion was lived out. The dominance of the Quraysh created the conditions necessary for a certain standardisation of local dialects and the growth of a common language of literary expression as manifested particularly in the *Mu'allaqāt* and the poetry of the sixth century CE. Rites and beliefs also tended to become more similar, while certain individuals found these circumstances conducive to their quest for forms of religious expression which were more relevant to the new situation with all its defects and negative aspects. Traditional forms of religion, linked to the tribal system (which was showing initial signs of breaking up), did not provide adequate spiritual sustenance.[11] A number of inhabitants of the Arabian Peninsula embraced Christianity, a proselytising religion, whereas Judaism considered itself the exclusive religion of the people of Israel and did not actively seek conversions. Its adherents were mainly in Yemen and in the region of Yathrib. Another group, known as the Ahnāf (plural of *hanif*: follower of the original, true monotheism), chose to abandon traditional polytheistic idol worship in favour of one sole God, the God of Abraham and Ishmael his son, the ancestors of the Arabs.

In other words, the period during which Islam initially developed was a period of change at many levels, and such periods by their very nature need figures to come forward bearing a message of great hope, opening up new horizons. Such was the mission of Muhammad ibn 'Abdallah.

2

The Preaching of Muhammad

C ompared with the founders of other religions, such as Confucius, Buddha, Zoroaster, Moses and Jesus Christ, Muhammad's life is relatively well documented, although the oldest existing historical elements have been in large part mingled with mythology, a dominant influence on traditional Arab and Islamic thought. Representations of the Prophet's personality and life draw on pre-Islamic examples of hagiography as well as examples from other civilisations, and introduce numerous mythical elements far removed from historical reality.[1] The only corrective to this tendency is what the Qur'an says of the Prophet. The Qur'an is constantly present in the lives of Muslims, and presents a rich human portrait, far removed from the idealised portrait to which Muslim sensibility inclined in subsequent eras, seeking a kind of union with the spiritual ideal which took on human form in the person of the Prophet.

However, historical details about Muhammad's childhood and youth are scarce and fragmentary, once one has stripped away the mythical elements added by subsequent generations. What is known about him can be summed up as follows: he belonged to Beni Hashim, one of the factions of the Quraysh, who played a significant symbolic role since some of their leaders from Qusayy onwards (in the sixth century CE) played an important role in the promotion of the pilgrimage to the Kaaba, escorting and accommodating pilgrims to the sanctuary. They did not have the same disposable material wealth as Beni Umayya, who had become wealthy through trade and thus played an influential role in Mecca and its environs.[2]

Muhammad was born in Mecca about 569 CE. He grew up an orphan, his father having died before Muhammad's birth. He spent a period of his childhood, as did other children of Qurayshi aristocratic families, with the Bedouin of Beni Huzan near Taef, acquiring a mastery of a pure form of Arabic, visiting his mother periodically with his nurse and accompanying her tribe in its nomadic existence and sedentary interludes. It seems that he went with her to the market of Ukkāz in the same period. For the period after the death of his mother while they were returning from Yathrib, there are only uneven fragments of information: his grandfather, 'Abd al Muttalib, adopted him for two years before he died, a responsibility that then passed to his son, Abu Tālib despite his straitened circumstances, Muhammad travelled frequently to Syria, once with his uncle, Abu Tālib, when he was ten years old, and once on one of Khadīja's trading missions when he was about twenty-four. He may also have travelled to Yemen, to the east of the Arabian Peninsula and perhaps Abyssinia.[3]

Although Muslim sensitivities have generally led them to shy away from recognising that Muhammad followed the religion of his tribe, the laws governing society impose this as the usual course for a child before he is able to choose and differentiate, imitating and following what he sees others doing, including the practice of their religion. Religion is an "all-embracing and coherent explanation of the universe, sustaining and propelling the lives of society and individuals".[4] It is not unlikely that Muhammad resembled his contemporaries by following existing forms of devotion, as attested by the following anecdote of Ibn Kalbi concerning 'Uzza, the goddess of the Quraysh mentioned in the Qur'an along with Lāt: "we have learnt that the Prophet mentioned her one day saying 'I sacrificed to 'Uzza a dust-coloured ewe and I follow the religion of my people'".[5] The offering of sacrifices to the gods was one of the manifestations of religious practice among the tribe of the Quraysh.

There are a number of first-hand accounts which, taken together, indicate that he was known for his piety, virtue and mild character. Perhaps he was introverted, like most orphans, without being cut off from normal social life.[6] His competence, qualities and, very possibly, his handsome bearing, were among the traits that endeared him to Khadīja bint Khawailad, the mature woman of strong personality whose graciousness Muhammad evoked until the end of his days despite the presence of other women. Khadīja, therefore, made an offer of marriage. The marriage produced a number of children; the male offspring died while the girls survived. The marriage was a decisive factor in determining the course of Muhammad's life, providing him with emotional and psychological stability and preserving him from poverty and hardship, and enabling him to dedicate himself to his mission when the divine call came. Khadīja gave him the moral support he needed in times of trial, and was the first to believe in him and adhere to his teaching, urging him to continue on the path of his destiny. On a personal and a social level, circumstances moulded Muhammad's personality, developing within him the confidence, the persuasiveness and charisma that set him apart from the very beginning of his preaching, and played a decisive role in the success of his mission despite all the obstacles in his path.

The point of view of the simple and trusting believer oscillates between, on the one hand, praising the ideal qualities of Muhammad, and, on the other hand, emphasising that he assumed the mantle of prophecy because of divine election and not because of his preparedness in human terms. Divine election does not necessarily preclude human predisposition, the difference being that the principle of divine election is accepted in faith without being able to prove it through rational arguments alone whereas propensity or readiness can be examined and tested empirically. It is doubtless for this reason that Muhammad Abduh gave the customary definition of revelation as being "the instruction that God communicates to his prophets by a rightful decree", then adopted another definition which met with his approval: "knowledge that the person discovers himself with the certainty that it is from God, through an intermediary or without an intermediary".[8] If such is the case, this knowledge does not take form overnight but develops progressively, and is influenced by personal, psychological and social elements. Prophetic inspiration can encompass all of these, blending and bonding them in such a way so that its components may be perceptible at certain moments, imperceptible at others.

The information that Muhammad gathered from his surrounding environment and on his journeys, from the *Aḥnāf*, as well as from Christians and Jews, was familiar to his contemporaries, although of little interest to them as they considered such matters to be beyond their intellectual horizons and far removed from their concerns. Muhammad also spent much time in meditation in the cave of Hira. All these elements matured within him, giving him the certainty that God had chosen him to communicate his message, first, to his own people and then, through them, to all others. Without a conscious effort, he made his own the spirit and questions of the time. When the revelation came upon him he was unprepared.

For that reason he was not immediately certain that God had chosen him to be the bearer of a momentous message, one that would bring upon him vexation and opposition. It may well be the case, as the *Sīra* relates, that he suffered from doubts when he was ordered to read, and needed the support of his wife Khadīja and her nephew, Waraqa ibn Nawfel.[9] Doubts haunted him again when the revelation was interrupted and tailed off, without his knowing whether or not the call addressed to him came from God or from one of the devils which populated the collective imagination. Society at that time recognised that what came over diviners, poets, magicians and "holy fools" (meaning those who were in constant contact with spirits, rather than those who were incapable of discernment) originated from contact with unseen forces which made them speak in a strange language. Muhammad, however, was not a diviner, or a poet, or a magician, or in contact with the world of the *junūn* (imperceptible, intelligent beings), nor was he a sage, rich in experience and reflection. He did not seek to bring about superficial changes in the way in which people related to one another in society or seek a position of leadership in his tribe or people. He was a Prophet, similar to the prophets of Israel, even if he was not afflicted by a loss of consciousness or fainting or fits or other symptoms of inner turmoil or unusual behaviour. Inspiration came upon him while he was awake and asleep, he did not speak of his own accord but by divine command, God addressed him through one of the angels: "truly this is the word of a noble Messenger having power, with the Lord of the Throne secure" (Sūra 81: 19–20), whom the Qur'an will subsequently identify as Gabriel (Sūra 2: 97), meaning the "strength of God".[10]

Therefore, the discourse that he heard and which weighed heavily upon him when it "came down upon his heart", according to the Qur'anic expression,[11] is the word of God which he conveys in human language, his word and word of God at the same time.[12] The word of God from the point of view of its source, human by its belonging to a particular language and its taking form in phrases and constructions according to the lexicon and grammar of the language and in the conceptual framework derived from the Prophet's culture and that of his milieu. It is noteworthy that Muslim scholars in the past were not averse to recording inspired declarations on the part of 'Umar or other Companions,[13] and took pains to prove the divine origin of such declarations. For we should not look at the minute particularities of what Muhammad could know or what was going through his or his Companions' minds, as what matters is the blending of his thoughts and aspirations to serve the aims that Divine Providence sought to realise through him. Historical and human influences and contingencies would have only documentary importance were they not, in their invisible dimension, an expression of something that transcends history. Is not the essence of belief a trust in this interior wisdom, a seeking of sustenance in its blinding illumination in the same way that one longs for the rays of the sun? The scientist, on the other hand, merely analyses the sun's rays dispassionately.

The *mutakallimūn* (theologians) were not generally concerned with the way in which the revelation was communicated, emphasising *taklīf* (obligation to observe religious precepts) and *'ibāda* (adoration). They concentrated instead on proving that the prophets could work miracles. The interpretation that acquired widespread currency in Islamic writings, for which Muslims cannot imagine an alternative, was that the revelation that descended on the Prophet consisted of words bearing a certain meaning. Most Muslims cannot imagine it otherwise. One of the sayings included by the prolific Egyptian scholar, al-Suyūti (849/1445–910/1505) in the *Itqān* is that Gabriel brought down to the Prophet the sense of the message; he learned these meanings and expressed them in the language of the Arabs.[14] He did not see this as somehow heretical or deviant. This point of view is perhaps the closest position to modern rationality and may serve as a starting point for a renewed examination of the question of inspiration, free from the constraints of traditional theories deriving their legitimacy from the majority support they enjoyed among scholars. Such an innovative approach would mean that the Qur'an retained its divine otherness, without the risk of anthropomorphism and, at the same time, its human aspect, its historicity and relativity. The two dimensions would not be separated, nor would either be inflated in importance or downplayed at the expense of the other, as tends to happen in the traditional Sunni vision, which minimises the Prophet's will and his innate qualities.[15] Is not the aim of the message of the Prophet to bring all people to participate in the divine experience which, in a distinctive way, was that of the Prophet? How can contemporary Muslims be forbidden from trying to explain, with their intellectual resources, matters about which revelation is silent? Do they not have the right to do what traditional scholars did when they tried to elucidate such questions, insofar as this was possible within their intellectual universe?

Muslim philosophers, using a certain number of terms existing in their culture, tried to explain the phenomenon of prophecy; philosophers, using a certain number of terms existing in their culture, tried to explain the phenom-

enon of prophecy; al-Kindi (*c.* 185/802–252/866), for example, considered that
the science of the prophets "was not a matter of research, mathematical schemes,
logic, or time, but depended rather on the will of the Almighty to purify and
enlighten their souls through righteousness, together with His assistance, inspiration, and messages". Al-Farābi (*c.* 259/872–339/950) used the categories of
Aristotelian metaphysics when he wrote:

> It is not impossible for the person whose imaginative powers were devel-
> oped to the utmost, to receive from the active intellect the partial essences
> of the present and future, or their imitations in sensible form, as well as the
> imitations of the different categories and all the superior beings, and that
> he perceive them.[16]

It is clear from the attempts of the philosophers that they were trying to
rationalise this central phenomenon in their religion and go beyond a viewpoint
of fideism or simple faith, but they did not find, in order to support their point
of view, any other concepts than those of purification, vision, a link between the
particular and active intelligence, or a kind of spiritual communication between
the human soul and the heavenly spheres enabling it to perceive therein the
images of events, in the same way that things are reflected on the surface of a
mirror.

What this shows is that Muslims in former times were not all convinced by
widely-held beliefs about prophecy, although they were not, in general, willing
to assume the consequences of a recognition that Muhammad played an active
role in transmitting the divine message, preferring a passive understanding of his
role: God speaks in human language and the angel communicates this in audible
form; God speaks and the angel translates into Arabic, then the Prophet hears
the message through the angel and in a mechanical fashion he communicates
what the angel has inspired. He plays no role in fashioning the message he is
ordered to communicate. They were led to this understanding by the Qur'anic
term "word of God", which had two different meanings: on the one hand, the
divine, transcendent quality of the message which cannot be encapsulated in any
human form without risking anthropomorphism; and, on the other hand, the
prophetic message itself, whose source is divine, but which is situated in time and
in space, transmitted by someone who is human in every respect, who thinks and
feels and imagines, hopes and despairs, is happy and angry and who is exposed

to unexpected events and contingencies in the same way as other humans. Their understanding of the term "God" was univocal, and they did not perceive that language has it limitations when communicating abstract terms. This leads in turn to its using expressions which communicate more than one meaning.

The Prophet was living in a world in which the sacred, or magic to use the Weberian[17] term, was omnipresent (as was the case for most of humanity until the seventeenth century CE), with divination and apparitions of supernatural beings dominating popular mentalities in cultures everywhere.[18]

That there are traces of these characteristics in what the Prophet communicated to his people and to Muslims is unsurprising. Whether from the point of view of faith or from a neutral historical viewpoint, the presence of such characteristics means only that God addresses his message to people in a language that they can understand; either the Prophet's revelation was vain, or he had to use what existed and was understood in his environment.[19] These elements are used in a way which transcends the limited historical context, reaching goals which were perhaps beyond what the contemporaries of the Prophet were prepared to accept. On this basis it is clear that the Prophet adopted without any qualms points of view held by his followers; the revelation gives them textual authority. For example, Al Barā' ibn Ma'rūr introduced the practice of turning toward the Kaaba instead of Syria before the revelation ordered the direction of the *qibla* (recess in a mosque indicating the direction of the Kaaba) to be changed.

When Muhammad arrived in Medina the Muslims were gathering for prayer without a call to prayer; he decided to make a horn similar to that used by the Jews for their call to prayer, then he gave up this idea. Then he ordered a bell to be made, which would be struck in order to bring the Muslims to prayer, before he accepted the opinion of Abdallah ibn Zaid ibn Thalaba, and gave Bilāl the task of calling the faithful to prayer in approximately the way which would become standard practice in the community.

'Abdallah ibn Jahash was the first to set aside a fifth of captured booty for the Prophet and shared out the rest when he attacked a caravan of the Quraysh in Nakhla, in the month of *Harām* (first month of the Islamic year). "Revelation came about what 'Abdallah ibn Jahash had done ..." It justified fighting in the month of *Harām* and recognised the division of the *fay'* (booty) in accordance with what the leader of the *sariyya* (expedition) decided personally should be done, following in all probability a practice already existing in pre-Islamic Arabia, distinguishing the requirements of a tribal sheikh from those of the

43

other participants in the razzia.[20] The book of the *Sīra* saw nothing wrong in recording this kind of incident and others of the same kind.

It is on the same basis that one should understand the way in which the Qur'an integrates stories of previous prophets and nations that had passed away. What it says about them is intended, in a didactic way, to explain to the Prophet's contemporaries how those who cast doubt on prophets announcing the One True God are punished, together with the need to turn away from their ancestral idols, as in the tales of the prophets and the Sūra of Hūd.

Muhammad was accused of receiving these tales from a non-Arabic speaker.[21] This accusation was intended to deny Muhammad's status as a prophet and to reject any idea of a special relationship between him and his Lord, which allowed him to learn things of which he had been unaware. The answer is provided by the revelation: "That is of the tidings of the Unseen that We reveal to thee; thou didst not know it, neither thy people before this" (Sūra 11:49) and "Not before this didst thou recite any Book" (Sūra 29:48). Muhammad had no knowledge of the supernatural world.[22]

Revelation, then, was the source of his knowledge. This was an exceptional state in which consciousness is lost, human capacities are suspended and the hidden depths of the unconscious become manifest, an overwhelming force that the Prophet cannot resist or govern by his own will; he conforms to what the divine will dictates to him, this revelation of the absolute, the invisible, the limitless; ordinary people cannot attain this state by their own, inevitably limited, rational capacities. It is emphasised once again that, at this level, there is no contradiction between the point of view of the believer and that of the scientific observer; the difference is only in their understanding of the origin of this overpowering force, not in its existence. The point of view of the believer attributes the origin of this overwhelming force to God, while the scientific observer merely gives an explanation of phenomena; the believer tries to answer two questions: "from where?" and "how?", while the scientist answers the question of how. The two points of view agree that Muhammad was honest and trustworthy when he said that he was not expressing his ideas but communicating a message from God.[23]

Modern research not only relies on the material context to explain history but also links these elements with the universe in all its dimensions and recognises that events may have a higher significance going beyond mere sense perception.

These stories, in any case, have a function which the revelation does not contest: it is to "strengthen the heart" of Muhammad: in today's language, to give him confidence in himself and in the truth of his message.[24] In his confrontation with those who accuse him of lying, he has only God's testimony that what he says is true and that what he announces has its origin in God.[25] So for that reason the revelation addresses him directly: "A book sent down to thee – let there be no impediment in thy breast because of it" (Sūra 7:2); he insists on many occasions that the revelation he receives is similar to that which the prophets received before him. He does not distinguish between the revelation they received and the revelation which concerned him and in which nobody else was associated: "We have revealed to thee as We revealed to Noah, and the Prophets after him, and We revealed to Abraham, Ishmael, Isaac, Jacob, and the Tribes, Jesus and Job, Jonah and Aaron, and Solomon' (Sūra 4:163), among other references.

He applies the same expressions to all the prophets without distinction ("bring down", "come", "inspire", "send", "choose", "warn", "announce", "exhort", "the Book", "evidence", "mention", "wisdom", "proofs", the "words" and the "messages" of God, the "way'", the "truth", the "prophet", the "envoy").[26]

The course and outcome of the prophecy of Muhammad was different from that of Moses and Jesus since the Torah was only codified many centuries after the death of Moses, following the Babylonian captivity. The Gospels were collected in various accounts of which only four were retained by the Church. Christ's message, stories of his life and his preaching were all mingled. The message of Muhammad was codified shortly after his death and a distinction made between the content of his message and what was biographical in nature. The Qur'an had guarantees of authenticity which did not exist in the case of the two previous prophecies. This does not, however, mean that there is a basic difference in the nature of the three messages and in the difficulties which arise when one deals with them, especially after the passage from the oral to the written form, from the Qur'an to the written text.

The Prophet time and again reminds his interlocutors that he has not introduced innovations, and that he follows the way of the prophets, those of the people of Israel, such as Abraham, and those such as Sālih, from the Arabic-speaking peoples.[27] What he has to communicate to them is a confirmation of the prophetic messages that they and the people of Israel have already received.[28] Had not God already recorded since the time of Moses "on the Tablets of everything an admonition, and a distinguishing of everything" (Sūra 7:145)? One should not, therefore, be surprised that monotheism in a pure form represents the heart of the message of all the prophets, and that righteousness constitutes the unchanging message of the prophets, in the same way that they called for the rejection of polytheism, oppression, pride and evil in general. There is no need to expand on this point, as it is well known that Muslims unanimously believe in the prophets who preceded Muhammad, even if there were attempts to establish a hierarchy among them. The Qur'an alluded to the existence of this order of precedence without elaborating. In particular, the Qur'an did not consider that the message of Muhammad abrogated or invalidated previous messages, considering that it authenticated them, enjoying a type of supremacy over them, although supremacy does not mean abrogation.

In this way it becomes apparent that the new message of Muhammad was a prolongation of previous monotheist messages, necessarily including elements from the culture of first/seventh century Mecca, as well as from Hejaz, the Arabian Peninsula and the wider Middle East. As it is addressed to people in a particular setting, this is only to be expected. It is clear that allusions to the *Junūn* (plural of *jinn*), the fall from Paradise and the role of *Iblis*, the devils, the angels, Noah and the Flood and other mythical elements, are derived from a traditional heritage which may seem today far removed from a contemporary worldview. The same is true of the myriad elements of wondrous fable and magic which do not have the same impact on a contemporary reader and are not understood in the same way.[29]

The presence of this kind of element should not, however, mean that another aspect of Muhammad's message be overlooked: the way in which it sets itself against prevailing beliefs and values. The same is true of the other prophetic messages. The Prophet's message takes existing realities as its starting point in order to change them and give them a new orientation, different from that which people had come to accept. The message may take account of generally accepted beliefs, but does not merely legitimise them. Had prophetic preaching not swept away prevailing beliefs inherited from the ancestors, beliefs which had become a natural part of dominant mentalities, had they not confronted clannish interests at a material and symbolic level, it would not be possible to account for the violent opposition which prophets (including Muhammad) encountered.[30] The radical, ground-breaking challenge of prophecy represents the very reason for its existence as well as for its spread, its continuity and its capacity to attract people of differing origins. As long as oppression and injustice exist, this will continue to be the case.

It is natural that prevailing opinions, values and morals did not fade away as soon as the Prophet's message appeared. As a reed bends in the wind without breaking or withering away, so too proponents of these traditional values and those whose interests were threatened by the Prophet's message waited for the storm to pass before rising up again, appearing on the surface in a new guise. They tried in particular to take advantage of situations of crisis and emergency and manipulate them for their own ends. At various times in the history of the Muslim community, these reactionary forces may even have enjoyed a degree of success, although at the expense of the lofty ideals of the original message, reduced at their hands to a backward-looking travesty.

3

Distinctive Characteristics of Muhammad's Message

Before studying the outcome of the preaching of Muhammad's message, it is initially worth examining a number of ways in which it has been interpreted, rectifying these interpretations and putting them in their correct context.

A religion, whatever its nature, cannot be reduced to its simple historical manifestation. However, that does not mean that it cannot be studied from an historical viewpoint. A distinction can be made between "open" and "closed" religion, to use the Bergsonian classification,[1] between the initial preaching and the forms of religiosity in which ritual plays an important part and fulfils various social functions designed to reinforce the bonds between individuals and impose a minimum of discipline. Social allegiances and solidarities have primacy over the truth, and priority is given to group cohesion rather than to the demands of individual conscience. It is in this context that one may reconsider the nature of the Prophet's message, cutting through confusion and obfuscation, using terms according to their original meaning and not that which they acquired over time due to various outside influences.

The first point to be underlined is the oral nature of the Prophet's discourse. Unlike those who were Companions of the Prophet for varying periods of time and who listened to him, neither present-day Muslims nor the generations who came after the "Followers" possess a direct knowledge of the specificities of this discourse, the precise circumstances surrounding it, the individual or individuals concerned, the aims of this discourse, or to other questions relating to each verse, group of verses, or *sūras* (chapters) of the Qur'an. It is true that the Qur'anic sciences include what is known as "circumstances of revelation", but the Companions of the Prophet were not concerned with these circumstances as they had lived through them. It was, in fact, subsequent generations who made an effort to examine the circumstances, and they were set down, albeit only partially, at a later period, at least two or three generations later. It is only natural that the text of the *asbāb en nuzul* is in parts marked by confusion and invention.[2]

The tone of the discourse, revealing pleasure or anger, admonition, warning, or censure, has also been lost. Words alone do not reveal this. It suffices to consider the different tones used when pronouncing a familiar expression such as "Good morning". The tone of voice can show whether the person is merely following the dictates of social convention, or is really pleased to be meeting the person he or she is greeting in the morning, or is angry because someone has arrived late, has been absent, or has forgotten something. Oral expression is also accompanied by facial expressions, a raising or a lowering of the voice and other similar means of communicating a message with a certain meaning. The context of discourse is, therefore, important although this is not reflected when discourse is codified in book form, and thus becomes subject, like texts in general and religious texts in particular, to varying and even contradictory interpretations. Variations in terminology play a part, as well as the variety of interests that may be at stake, together with the influence of temperament and mentality. Finally, a specific tradition, or group of competing traditions, take on a more or less fixed form, striving to secure a dominant position for an exclusive interpretation which is considered to be authentic.

The term "Qur'an" should really be used only for the message which the Prophet conveyed orally to his contemporaries. As far as what was collected after his death in a particular order "between two covers" is concerned, it is known that the Prophet's Companions were not initially in agreement about the legitimacy of this collection which the Prophet did not carry out or personally order. Omar ibn al Khattab, for example, opposed Abu Bakr on this subject before "God enlightened his heart" on the initiative of his adviser. They were hesitant even about what name to give to the document before they agreed on the term *mushaf* (volume, book), a term they had encountered in Abyssinia, according to the chroniclers.[3] The various transmitted versions were unified by a political decision taken at the period of 'Uthmān; agreement was reached on a unified *mushaf*, while unofficial *mushafs* were burnt for fear that Muslims would disagree about their sacred text in the same way as did the Jews and the

Christians.[4] The Ethiopian Church, in particular, familiar to the first Muslims, is the only Church to consider the Book of Enoch and the Jubilees as canonical. During the rule of Marwān ibn Hakam (64/684–65/685), the *mushaf* of Hafsa, the wife of the Prophet, was burnt after her death. The contemporary historian may regret the irrevocable loss of these documents, while also recognising that the move toward a standard text had, incontestably, a salutary effect: were it not for this the Muslim community might have been slow to agree on a unified text, with the possibility of divisions arising as result of this delay, divisions graver than those which the community experienced at the end of 'Uthmān's reign. The question of political power was never entirely absent, as the Islamic state's existence and legitimacy derived from religion. State and religion interacted in both negative and positive ways.

In any case, the only logical conclusion is that the "reminder" that God undertook to perpetuate was the content and not the outer form, the content of Muhammad's preaching, his proclamation, admonishment and guidance, rather than the expressions and words used from which the message was moulded, set down in a particular form and attributed to a particular people. This outer linguistic form has grammar, syntax and grammatical bases which are no different from those of any other language. The Prophet himself did not prohibit his Companions from varying their styles of reading aloud in public verses which they had memorised; all were considered licit, although some Companions adhered rigidly to the style that they had heard the Prophet using, considering a multiplicity of styles to be a deformation of God's Word.[5]

When the Qur'an challenged unbelievers to produce ten sūras or even one sūra rivalling the Qur'an, this is not because it is wondrously inimitable due to its style and rhetorical characteristics, but because of its divine origin, unattainable for most people; only the prophets and the divine envoys are privy to its mysteries. There is no doubt that the style of the Qur'an is distinct, unique and distinguished, and anyone reading it or listening to it is conscious of its unique status. However, great works of art, be they poetry, prose, drawings, sculptures, or musical masterpieces, are all, in their particular way, unique. They cannot, despite their human origins, be reproduced. They can, however, be imitated if someone has the necessary gifts and capabilities, and imitation always represents a decline when compared with the original created work. If a new creation is truly equivalent to the original, this means that it is, in fact, a new creation, far removed from a copy or an imitation.

As far as the Qur'an is concerned, from where could potential imitators derive the power given to the prophets alone? Certain early Mu'tazilites put forward the idea of *sirfa*, that is to say, that God averted human hearts from the possibility of producing another Qur'an: the Qur'an, insofar as it is stylistically distinctive, is not beyond human capability simply because of its distinct language.[6] Most Muslim scholars hold the view that the inimitability (*i'jāz*) of the Qur'an is located in its style and form and what has been called since the time of 'Abd al-Qāhir al-Jurjānī (d. 473/1081), *nazm*, that is, the coherence and balance of the text. This tendency can be explained by their insistent attempts to demonstrate the truthful sincerity of the Prophet and the way in which the central tenets of Islam could stand up to empirical examination. However, the divine origin of the text cannot be proved by rational means, leaving faith or unbelief as the only possible choices. This tends to invalidate the competence of the theologians in its traditional form at least.

Muslims generally believe that the authenticity of their sacred text is guaranteed by the strict rules governing its memorisation and by the precautions taken at the time of the collection and recording of the text. Certain Muslims claim that this is a particularity of the Qur'an, although Orthodox Jews maintain the same is true of the Torah. Archaeological excavations in Palestine and serious research show that the events related in the Torah do not have a factual basis, and that they are an ideologically-based construction dating from the period of the Babylonian exile in the sixth century BCE and the discovery by the Jews of a cultural world infinitely richer than their own. When they returned from exile and began to compose their own religious texts, they re-worked the foundation myths widespread across the region.[7] Orthodox Jews cling to the details of rites and prohibitions transmitted in the Torah and in the rabbinical commentaries.

Official teaching of Christian Churches until recent times followed the same trend, and fundamentalist Protestant Churches in particular still believe today in the literal truth of all the details contained in the Bible, covering the origins of humankind (they believe that the first man, Adam, appeared a few thousand years ago, not five million years as modern science has shown), the history of the world, and the most basic moral rules.[8]

Confusion often also arises (in the context of discussion about the Qur'an) about the meaning of the term "book", with many people believing that this means what is generally understood by the term "book", that is to say, what is inscribed in the form of a written line on a supporting surface, be it a rock, bone, papyrus, parchment, paper, or any other material support. The term Qur'an does not have this meaning at all when it refers to the Book in general, or the written Book, the "Book of God", the "mother of books", the book that was revealed to Muhammad or to the other prophets and divine messengers, or the "precious books" which are within the "immaculate pages" that the Prophet recites, or the "People of the Book".[9] All these terms refer not to the material book which the reader can touch, transcribe, open and close at a particular page, put in a store-room or on a shelf, but rather to the content of the message that God saw fit to entrust to the prophets in order that they could communicate it to humankind, encouraging them to be righteous in every way, guiding them toward what is good for their lives and their destinies. There is no clearer proof for this than the way in which the revelation used the term "Book" when the Prophet had not received the complete Qur'an, revealed in instalments, at intervals of varying length. One should not forget that the roles of writing and reading can vary from one society to another; reading in the Arab setting, as was also the case for the Ancient Greeks and other societies, was an oral, public event: one person read while others listened, engaging in debate. There was no readily available text in the material sense. This would become available only in the second/eighth century when Chinese-inspired techniques of producing paper became known and the book in the accustomed sense of the word entered general circulation. In addition, Arabic writing at the time of the Prophet lacked points and vowel indications, and it was thus difficult to rely on a written text as a vehicle for trans-mitting the content of a message. It is an exaggeration to claim that the Qur'an alone is the word of God. According to the logic of revelation, the Qur'an is the "copy", taking into account prevailing conditions at the time of Muhammad and the existing intellectual and cultural context.

The same is true of the question of the word of God. All those who have even a slight knowledge of the history of Islamic intellectual developments have heard of the heated debates that took place during the Abbāsid period between philos-ophers, jurists and hadīth specialists. In the third/ninth century the holders of political power entered the fray, at the time of the Caliphs al-Ma'mun, Mu'tasim, Wathiq and al-Mutawakkil, then in the fifth/eleventh century at the time of al-Qādir (381/991–422/1031), in order to secure the victory of one or other of the competing factions, thus promoting what they perceived as their interests. One such question was the created status of the Qur'an: was it, as the Word of God, created, or uncreated?[10] Another question was the Ash'arite distinction between the interior word (*nafsi*) and the written word (*lafzi*). Muslims at that time realised the difficulties involved in proving the divine origin of Muhammad's message without falling into the trap of anthropomorphism or reification of the Word of God, but they did not take account of the way in which divine revelation used human expressions to convey transcendent truths which the Qur'an itself says cannot be enumerated, let alone contained in a material "receptacle" of whatever kind: "Say: if the sea were ink for the Words of the Lord, the sea would be spent before the Words of my Lord are spent, though we brought replenishment the like of it."[11] Nor did they realise that what was meant by the term "Qur'an" was not the discourse emanating from Muhammad himself but the content of the message that God wanted to communicate and which he described thus: "It is surely a noble Qur'an, in a hidden book none but the purified shall touch; a sending down from the Lord of all Being."[12] Here, as on numerous occasions, they took what could be empirically observed as the benchmark by which the unknown and mysterious workings of Providence could be studied, and thus imposed necessarily limited human categories and interpretations on the domain of the divine. This created a tendency toward anthropomorphism and other elements at which we shall look in due course.

In order to avoid confusing abstract, invisible realities and tangible human realities situated in space and time, as though what is valid for one is valid for the other, one ought to be aware of the literary style of divine revelation, based on metaphor, allusion, suggestion and the use of proverbs so that the listener may grasp the intended message and adhere to it. Nor should the specific nature of mythical discourse be misunderstood and read as though it were related to, and in conformity with, conceptual discourse. The specialists in *tafsīr* went to great lengths in order to explain all the details of the most sweeping and general declarations, and to specify what was meant by every allusion. Symbols became tangible historical facts. It is not the commands and prohibitions relating to prevailing circumstances at the time of Muhammad's preaching which should be studied, but their implicit aims and intentions. Observing inconsistencies between the orders and the interdictions, intended as they are for guidance and orientation, is not a new trend; scholars have traditionally endeavoured to go beyond perceived incompatibilities or contradictions using the notion of *naskh*, or abrogation of certain verses. This is a meaningful approach only when it draws attention to the need to take account of new situations which may arise: this is an approach contrary to that of the fundamentalists.

The question of textual interpretation is central, and from the second/eighth century onwards, Muslims adopted a literal approach to interpretation of the Qur'an. This period saw the development of *fiqh* and was also a time when the state became concerned with the organisation of society on a religious basis. It was also the period when the Qur'anic text was definitively established. Without going in to the details about the tendency to give one verse primacy over another, through subjective interpretation and text-twisting, and the way in which precepts (to use the jurists' appellation) were based on hadīths authenticated by one commentator rather than on Qur'anic verses, one can conclude that *fiqh* and its findings were part of the obligations of religion for Muslims for many centuries. It began to seem less self-evident in modern times, under the pressure of the many profound changes affecting Muslim societies.

Four main contemporary trends can be identified:

(1) The position defended by the majority of scholars who have received a traditional training, which is a prolongation of the position traditionally taken by Muslims entailing, on the level of theory, standing by the traditional system, while, at the practical level of application, accepting that this system be violated. They consider it necessary for subjects to submit to the will of the ruler, even a tyrannical one, to the extent of obeying his edicts even if their link with *fiqh* is tenuous or non-existent. These scholars, even if they cling to traditional schemas, are unaware of the role played by *fiqh* at the time of its early development. They are equally unaware that the new context and its stakes are very different from those of the past. Many of these individuals are defending their personal or factional interests: this is legitimate enough, but at that point religion becomes a means of camouflaging these interests. The defence of religion is not, therefore, the main motive of those who proclaim themselves to be its heralds and champions.

(2) The position of the contemporary Salafite movements and various thinkers aware of the need to go beyond traditional solutions. They do not reject the legislative aspect of the Qur'an, while recognising that precepts and prescriptions, particularly about interpersonal rights and duties, can evolve if the circumstances surrounding the original judgment have changed. Most of the leaders of the Reform movement from Muhammad Abduh (1261/1849–1323/1905) onwards, such as Tahar Haddad (1306/1889–1354/1935) in Tunisia, Ben Badis (1306/1889–1358/1940) in Algeria and Allāl al Fāsi (1328/1910–1393/1974) in Morocco, have held this position. This conciliatory position was audacious in the

context of the early twentieth century, and is undeniably more progressive than that of the traditionalist *sheikhs*. This position does not present a fundamental solution to the basic dilemma, as its theoretical base is weak. Its supporters are few and the fundamentalist tide has marginalised them.

(3) For contemporary Islamist movements, it is unthinkable to resign oneself to accepting the distance that has opened up between the Qur'an and everyday reality; reality must be changed and the golden age of the early Muslim community restored. The text is not to be subjected to the test of quotidian reality. This position is based on a sort of unhistorical wishful thinking, even if its internal logic is more structured. It has attracted many young people and the oppressed and anxious in society, victims of failed modernisation. However, its theoretical base is weak, and its adherents include many uneducated propagandists.

(4) Mahmoud Muhammad Taha (1908–85) was alone in defending the point of view expressed in his book, *ar-risāla atthāniya min al islām*, and it cost him his life.[13] Taha maintained that the message of Muhammad was a general message directed toward humankind at the Meccan period, while in the period at Medina it was directed toward the contemporaries of the Prophet. It follows then that particular judgments relevant to the historical circumstances of people at the beginning of the seventh century were no longer appropriate to their situation in the second half of the twentieth century. What was needed was a return to the universal message which remains valid despite changed circumstances.[14]

Each of these points of view can be justified and, according to one's viewpoint, each has elements of validity. Their proponents see themselves as pragmatic, seeking ways of extricating the Muslim community from decadence and backwardness. In general they lack the appropriate theoretical basis with which to confront the questions facing them. These theoretical resources are as yet still caught up in secondary questions, and have not reached the level of argumentation and dialectic. History is still seen as immobile, and dynamics and movement go unnoticed.

With regard to traditional scholars, their position is manifestly weak. They are unable to provide coherent responses, while the Utopian vision of the Islamist movements has no chance of success. It would condemn Muslim societies to being overtaken by the movement of history and its complexities, far removed from the simplicity of the early Muslim community. The values of the Enlightenment, far from being rejected, are becoming more firmly established. The points of view of Mahmoud Muhammad Taha and the Islamic reformers converge in that both call for part of the message of Muhammad to be retained, while the rest will be set aside or interpreted, without any guarantee that a particular interpretation is more valid than its rivals.

4
Legislation

The first observation would be that revelation does not speak in terms of the Sharīʿa as a divine law; it speaks of it as a way[1] for the believer to follow.[2] From this point of view it is a binding commitment. The actual details of conduct are only sketched out; they are solutions to particular challenges facing the community at a given moment. This is why the solutions are diverse, reflecting as they do the variety of situations arising. Most questions, relating either to conditions prevailing at the time of Muhammad or to subsequent eventualities, are not explicitly addressed in any given text.

These guidelines are essentially of a moral and educational nature and were present from the Meccan period onwards. They concern questions of liturgical practice, although they cannot be separated from the main thrust of divine revelation at that period: God's unity, resurrection, reward and punishment for deeds committed, and the prophetic missions. Prayer, alms-giving, good deeds, truth, patience, forbearance, devoutness, faithfulness and loyalty, chastity, freeing slaves, caring for orphans, the destitute and prisoners, giving their due to family members and strangers alike: revelation gave priority to these questions during the Meccan period, while forbidding murder, injustice and aggression, tyranny and abuse of power, depravity and fornication, lies and defamation, squandering and hoarding of wealth, greed and miserliness, cavilling and backbiting, the chiding of beggars and the exploitation of orphans. All of these moral guidelines and prohibitions are signposts on the way the believer must follow. There is no difference between these elements and fasting, pilgrimage, the direction to take for prayer, combat in God's cause, marriage, divorce and theft, and other concerns of divine revelation during the Medinan period.

Mahmoud Taha's separation of the Meccan and the Medinan stages of Muhammad's preaching seems unconvincing, nor is it possible to interpret each of the so-called "prescriptive verses" in isolation from the others, from their historical context and from the Qur'anic text as a whole. The *fuqahā'* (plural of *faqīh*: specialist in jurisprudence) throughout history have done precisely this. *Al-ahkām* is an Islamic legal term indicating, in a descending order, what is obligatory, recommended, licit, reprehensible and prohibited. These distinctions have no basis in the Qur'anic message. Muhammad's preaching concerns what was good and evil at the moment of the revelation. The orientations given are the basic elements from which Muslims will deduce the criteria of good conduct and sound morals. This does not mean a slavishly literal observation of the text, rather a search for its spirit and aims. God alone will be worshipped, and each individual's conscience will be the first and final arbitrator in determining their response to God's initiative.

This reading of the text of the Qur'an will ensure that the message of Islam is credible wherever Muslims find themselves. With regard to what the Qur'an says about Adam, Eve, *Iblīs*, *jinn*-s, demons, angels and prophetic miracles, the believer will readily perceive that these stories are produced by a mentality which lends credence to myth. He or she can see them as symbols and allegories of a deeper message, not historical fact. Muslims will also readily accept interpretations of the Qur'anic rules relating to worship and social relations (on the few occasions where detailed texts exist) which recognise the influence of the simple way of life at the time of the Prophet in the region of the Hejaz, where relations between individuals were simpler than in other settings, especially modern societies in the Arab world and the West.

The voluminous writings which consumed the energies of generations of 'ulamā' (plural of *'alīm*: religious scholar) should be left aside and the recommendations of the Qur'an concerning ritual prayer examined. The Qur'an deliberately avoids stipulating the number of prayers and how to carry them out. Little precision is given to the inner intentions of the person praying, to ritual purity, ablutions, upright posture, recital of the *Fātiha* (first sūra of the Qur'an), a verse or collection of verses, bowing, prostration and the concluding invocation. Nor are there detailed allusions to the number of bows, which can vary from one prayer to another, and the different role of imāms and the ordinary believer in communal prayer.[3] It is clear that the traditions concerning the number of prayers imposed on the occasion of the *mi'irāj* (nocturnal journey of the Prophet to the seven heavens) and the famous incident when the Prophet and God haggled over the number of prayers (reduced from fifty to five on the recommendation of Moses) are produced by a mentality prone to believing in myths, and lack all credibility. What is important is that the Prophet prayed in a certain manner and that Muslims imitated him.[4] Muslims everywhere are not, however, obliged to follow this down to the last detail, even supposing that there was a unified, unchanging method of praying during the Prophet's lifetime. Were this the case, that would mean that the inhabitants of the Polar regions, where the summer day is so long as to leave almost no night (in winter the contrary is true) are less concerned by the teaching of Muhammad than the inhabitants of temperate regions where there is not a major difference between the length of day and the night whatever the season. The same could be said of those living in industrialised societies where machines impose lifestyles and work practices totally different from those existing in nomadic, agricultural and trading societies, or any people whose styles of life differ radically from simple traditional forms of life.[5]

The historian may observe that certain rites were already familiar at the time of the revelation of Islam, such as ablutions (which existed in Jewish communities although in a different form), the upright posture for prayer (a practice of the Syriac Church), prostrations and bowing.[6] That in no way diminishes the importance of the divine command to pray, or the need for each believer to periodically observe moments of retreat and meditation, and interrupt quotidian activities to humbly examine his or her conscience. This is not to contest the value of the five daily prayers, Friday prayer, or prayers on the occasion of the two great feasts, *Eid el kabīr* and *Eid es-saghīr*, at funerals and so on. Prayers on these occasions remain the ideal formula for two types of believers: those who believe that these prayers are obligatory and binding in their traditional form; and those who live in a setting which allows them to pray in the time-honoured manner. What of other believers who may have drifted away from the practice of their religion, or who struggle between ideals and the realities of life: should they too not have the right to adhere to the precepts of their religion without having necessarily to follow the teaching of bygone generations down to the very last detail?

The same is true of alms-giving, as the Qur'an did not determine the amount or specify the exact purpose for which it was intended. The basic principle remains valid: the duty of solidarity between rich and poor. Alms-giving should not be considered simply on the basis of the types of financial resources and the ways of using them which existed in the first/seventh century. Such an approach betrays narrow-mindedness and ignorance both of the aim of alms-giving and of modern forms of solidarity which represent a progress in comparison with traditional forms of largesse and munificence. These modern forms may well be closer to the spirit of Muhammad's teaching according to which the poor have a right to share in the resources of the rich.[7] The form that these resources take has evolved as well as the means of accumulating and disposing of them, and new forms of solidarity respect the needy and offer them assistance in ways which were non-existent in traditional societies, although considered today as essential human rights: education, employment, shelter, medical attention and so on.

Previous research has demonstrated how the Ramadhan fast was recommended by the Qur'an in various forms: "Believers, fasting is decreed for you as it was decreed for those before you" (Sūra 2:183), "to fast is better for you" (Sūra 2:184), and "Therefore whoever of you is present in that month, let him fast" (Sūra 2:185).[8] The possibility of not fasting, and replacing the fast by donations of food to the poor was left open and verses such as "For those of you who can afford it there is a ransom: the feeding of a poor man" and "Allah desires your wellbeing, not your discomfort" (Sūra 2:184–5), were interpreted only as forbidding the substitution of the fast with food gifts after the death of the Prophet. During his lifetime the practice was acceptable. Muslims today are often uneasy when they directly encounter the text of the Qur'an, and their reading of it is heavily influenced by the voluminous centuries-old commentaries of the *fuqahā'* and the *tafsīr* (Qur'anic interpretation) scholars. It is, therefore, unsurprising that they find themselves in a dilemma: they merely comply with prevailing custom and put on an appearance of fasting. This is far from being the original aim of the fast. They can also try to devise casuistic solutions out of expediency: the authors of certain *fatwas* (formal legal opinions) suggest that the inhabitants situated to the north or south of a particular line of latitude (45th parallel) must observe the timetable foreseen for this latitude, without considering the time at which the sun rises and sets.[9]

It is also common knowledge that the pilgrimage was one of the pre-Islamic rites practised by the Arabs. Islam adopted it and conferred upon it a new meaning within the context of monotheism. It is incontestable that the rites of the pilgrimage retain the residues of age-old mythology, in particular the stoning of devils and offering of sacrifices. This is undeniably a way to release pent-up emotions, canalising violence in a harmless way. Is it a binding obligation today for Muslims who may be unhappy with such practices and who nevertheless feel compelled to go through with them? Is it not right in this case for each believer to be honest with themselves rather than simply perform rituals without any personal convictions? These questions connected with the "pillars" (*arkān*) of Islam have not been raised deliberately to try to trouble religious sensitivities. Those who feel that they have to adhere to the prescriptions of the *fuqahā'* should do what they hold to be binding; it is not for us or anyone else to minimise the important emotional dimension involved in any act of prayer or liturgy. These cannot be altered easily by the will of an individual or of a group, nor is it systematically desirable. One can observe, however, an increasing drift away from traditional rituals: people do not contest the "pillars" of Islam in general terms, it is simply that society has changed radically and the experience of previous generations seems remote. Identifying problems and seeking acceptable solutions does not necessarily indicate a deliberate trawling through murky waters, as it were, creating purely imaginary difficulties. Ghazāli, in his *Ihyā' 'ulūm ed-dīn*, urges individual Muslims repeatedly to "consult your heart". This could be a suitable starting point for Muslims as they try to bridge the gap between religion and daily life, shaking off the tendency to imitate blindly in the absence of any valid justification. Honesty is a basic condition of religious practice, as well as being an integral part of personal balance and well-being. The person who chooses to speak the truth must be able to express his or her deepest aspirations without suffering any harm or becoming a scapegoat, and this happens only when freedom is respected and does not become a bargaining counter.

In the light of these observations about ritual practices, Qur'anic injunctions and interdictions, necessary in the context of the social conditions prevailing in the first/seventh century, begin to take on less problematic proportions. The Qur'an should be treated as a whole, without isolating a limited number of verses. Readers should be attentive to the intention behind the text, as well as to the reasons which led Muslims in the past to adopt the interpretation that they did. Less reliance should be placed on a mere tenth of the more than 6,000 verses in the Qur'an, without counting repetitions. A large proportion of the text is of a narrative rather than prescriptive character.[10] The content of the Qur'anic text represents only a small proportion of the prescriptions set out by the *fuqahā'*, who nevertheless claimed that they had deduced them from the Qur'an using methods that were free from error. It is more important for a contemporary reader to take account of changing circumstances, particularly with regard to the details of personal conduct. This includes such matters as the law of talion (retaliation in kind) in case of injury or aggression, in keeping with Jewish practice, and the forbidding of images, a practice that may have been justified in the first/ seventh century given that pagan idol worship was a recent phenomenon. In modern society, dominated by the image in various forms, this interdiction seems to have lost its *raison d'être*.

Slavery is not a question high on the contemporary agenda. The Qur'an did not order its abolition, despite urging that slaves should be released and creating numerous opportunities and means of putting an end to this practice which is contrary to human dignity. Other questions weighing on the conscience of the community of believers need urgent solutions, as they are sources of conflict and tragedy which can result in innocent blood being shed. Such questions include apostasy, the application of the law of talion, theft, interest-generating loans, the relationship between state and religion and the organisation of family life.

The question of apostasy may be considered first. The Qur'an contains no allusion to a physical punishment to be inflicted on the apostate. It mentioned only a sanction in the next world which no human agent can administer. Curiously, many Muslims, including those who are thought to be expert in questions of faith, think that punishing apostates is a divine command simply because of an unreliable *hadīth*: "Kill the person who changes his religion", taking Abū Bakr, who killed those described as "apostates" (or *ahl al ridda*), as an example. It is equally singular that archaic practices prevail over the principle of religious freedom contained in Muhammad's message, a principle to be applied without exception or hesitation.[11] It is as though there is an apprehension that non-application of the death penalty for apostasy will somehow lead simple folk to think that someone who leaves the Muslim community does so because their experience of Islam was an unhappy one. This will lead others to do the same, and thus reduce the number of Muslims! It is as though the touchstone of belief is external compliance and not interior conviction and free choice. Strange as it may seem, this is the fate of every prophetic message which suffers interpretations influenced by social or historical conditions which divert it from its aims. On grounds of fidelity, the essential message of a religion is contradicted.[12]

As far as retributive killing is concerned, it is evident that every legal system, irrespective of its origins, punishes the crime of murder. The Qur'anic text stipulates that the punishment for killing is death, a sanction limited to the assassin alone, to the exclusion of any of his kinsfolk. The way is left open for pardon to be granted by the victim's relations. This constitutes a recognition of the principle of individual and not communal punishment. It also goes beyond an automatic application of the sanction, contradicting subsequent decisions taken by the *fuqahā'.* It also shows that retaliatory killing is not an end in itself but is a way of dealing with the harsh realities of human existence. Substituting capital punishment with imprisonment or other sanctions does not mean contradicting the Qur'anic principle in general. In modern times, it is the state alone which can legally use violent means when dealing out punishments on various classes of offender. Formerly, in the context of a tribal system and in the absence of state institutions, the family of the victim could take matters into their own hands. There is no reason for not going further and abolishing capital punishment, especially in the complex setting of modern urban life where there is no guarantee that errors will not be made when passing judgment, leading to innocent lives being lost. If the accused person's life is spared, there remains a possibility of rectifying such errors. In the case of a capital sentence, this is impossible. It is difficult to believe that the Muslim conscience would tolerate the sacrifice of an innocent person because of an obstinate adhesion to outmoded forms of punishment that may have had their justification in traditional societies.

Some Muslims, relying on a supposedly categorical text, hold that that the amputation of a thief's hand is a divine command concerning which there is no room for interpretation.[13] Research has shown that commentators and scholars have long debated the precise meaning of the terms "cut", "hand", and the importance of the theft which leads to punishment by amputation.[14] They stipulate that the term "theft" is restricted to property which has been placed under protection and in which the thief has no share, such as public funds. Certain commentators sought judicial loopholes to try to avoid applying this sanction. This approach characterised Sunni Muslim thought: one is supposed to respect a lofty but theoretical ideal, while in practice accepting ways around it that are often far removed from idealistic theory. This punishment is not applied for a number of possible reasons: either it goes against prevailing practices, or people's consciences will not tolerate it. If the question can be considered in a socio-historical light, Muslims will perhaps be able to avoid this kind of uncomfortable double standard.

There is no doubt that this kind of punishment existed in the pre-Islamic period, and, as in all nomadic societies based on subsistence economies, it is only natural that theft should be punished severely as this type of crime put the victim's very existence in jeopardy. It may be that draconian punishment of that kind was the only way to maintain a minimum of law and order in the absence of a political authority whose sway extended over society as a whole. Physical punishment in the form of beating, flogging and amputation were current as was capital punishment, and it was difficult to envisage any alternative guarantee of social stability. Qur'anic recommendations were in keeping with the prevailing situation in the first/seventh century, although this does not mean that the possibility of other forms of sanction should be excluded as society evolves and adopts values in keeping with its evolution. All forms of corporal punishment and torture have come to be considered as a denial of human dignity. In other words, sanctions of any kind (including the amputation of a thief's hand), are not ends in themselves. They can be discarded and replaced by others more in keeping with the conditions in which modern Muslim societies live, as long as they fulfil the ultimate aim of guaranteeing social stability by other means. The abolition of these punishments in the vast majority of Muslim countries has not led their inhabitants to deviate from the spirit of the Prophet's teaching. Their application even today, on the pretext of applying the Shari'a, is the object of growing condemnation, particularly on the part of concerned and aware Muslims. This was what Muhammad Iqbal (1290/1873–1356/1938) meant when he said over seventy years ago: "The primary source of the law of Islam is the Quran. The Quran is not a legal code. Its main purpose is to awaken in man the higher consciousness of his relation with God and the universe." He went on:

> The prophet's method is to train one particular people and to use them as a nucleus for the building of a universal Shari'at. In doing so he accentuates the principles underlying the social life of mankind of human life and applies them to concrete cases in the light of the specific habits of the people before him. The Shari'at values resulting from this application (e.g. rules relating to penalties for crimes) are in a sense specific to that people. Since their observance is not an end in itself they cannot be imposed in their exact form on future generations.[15]

The question of interest-generating loans (usury) also seems to be moving toward resolution. At the heart of the problem lies the question of whether transactions with banks and similar institutions involving interest-generating loans can be classed as usury. Two points need to be made here, first, both Christianity and Judaism forbid usury, although today their adherents no longer consider this interdiction as applying to interest-generating loans and borrowing. Secondly, the absolute ban on usury mentioned in numerous verses of the Qur'an applies to loans on which huge rates of interest are charged. This meant that one of the parties involved in the transaction was enriched without making any effort at the expense of the other, who was reduced to poverty because of the need for money at a particular point in time. In addition, non-payment of the debt, at this extortionate rate of interest, could lead to the enslavement of the debtor. For these reasons, the Qur'anic ban on usury is quite natural, and can be justly applied to all cases where this kind of excess and illegal exploitation occurs.

Borrowing from a bank and paying interest on the loan does not come into the category of forbidden activities. First, it is not a transaction involving two individuals, but rather a person, on the one hand, and a banking institution, on the other hand. At the time of the Prophet such institutions did not exist and it is difficult to imagine the prohibition of something that did not exist. Secondly, the interest levied by the bank does not amount to usury: it is at a rate set by the state in advance taking into account the rates of inflation, the cost of financial operations, the taxes paid by the bank and the revenue generated by the sum that has been borrowed. The consequences too are very different from those of usury, and include giving an impetus to economic activity and generating of productive projects. This said, the distress suffered by the poor in Muslim countries (and non-Muslim countries such as India) when they are obliged to borrow from moneylenders is glaringly obvious. The institutions which could set out their rights and responsibilities are absent from the scene.

One thus returns again to the general principle of considering the reasons behind what is commanded and forbidden by the Qur'an, and the underlying wisdom of their teachings rather than the particular form they assumed at the time of the revelation. This is preferable to the manoeuvring of so-called "Islamic banks" which receive the blessing of certain official religious bodies. These banks are Islamic only in name and the interest charged on their loans (not described as such in order to disguise them) can be higher than that of ordinary banks. This favours those managing the banks more than it does their gullible customers.[16]

Dealing with banks has become normal practice in Islamic countries, involved as they are in financial transactions governed by the law. The conscience of the Muslim community does not see anything wrong with these secular transac-

tions. Things are very different when it comes to political decision-making and
the family. In modern societies it is these two institutions which are the most
resistant to secularisation; religion plays an important legitimising role in these
institutions. It is difficult to change or suppress this dimension which has existed
for generations. In reality, deriving political authority from divine right has
traditionally functioned in conservative religious mentalities as a guarantee of
stability and as a means of gaining support from a willing populace. Were it not
for this divine right, why would a ruler be more competent than anyone else to
legally use violent means for the administration of society and for dealing with
inevitable conflicts? This solution was convenient for both ruler and subject,
and the first contestations developed only when nation states grew up out of
the rubble of the old empires. These states generally had stable borders and its
citizens were subject to a unified legal code.

This historical dimension is often overlooked by the proponents of an
abstract view of religion and its so-called "essence". They consider that the
separation between religion and state in modern Western societies is somehow
due to the innate nature of the Christian faith widespread in these societies.[17] In
their opinion Christianity believes that Caesar should be given what is Caesar's
and God that which is His. Christ exercised no political authority in contrast to
the Prophet who, from the very beginnings of Islam, held out of necessity both
spiritual and temporal power. In making this claim, they betray their ignorance
of the many conflicts in Christian countries between church and state, and the
subsequent exclusion of clerics from political life. At the same time they are
unaware of the reality of political power as exercised by Muslim rulers and their
links with the men making up the religious establishment. In the light of Ibn
Khaldoun's analysis of the nature of the different kinds of sovereign power it is
not necessary to go into details about the way in which authority was exercised
throughout history in Muslim states.

Of primary concern is the link between the preaching of Muhammad and
his actions during the period between his departure from Mecca for Medina
and his death. During this period of about ten years the Prophet himself
commanded a number of military expeditions and dispatched his Companions on other such expeditions. He was the unchallenged leader of this small
nucleus of followers who were at the origin of a vast Muslim empire. He was
also the ultimate arbitrator in the various disputes arising among Muslims in
different fields. It is necessary to clarify his attitude in the following areas: his

use of violent means; his leadership in the Muslim community; and the role of
adjudication in disputes, and to examine their significance in the context of the
time. Did Muhammad consistently instigate violence? Was he not driven to do
this by the Quraysh who threatened the very existence of the incipient Muslim
community? The Quraysh perceived the new religion as a threat to their trading
interests and a potential death-blow to the system on which these interests were
based. A whole range of methods were employed to win over the followers of the
Prophet, followed by active persecution. Muhammad had no other choice but
to break the bonds of tribal solidarity uniting his opponents, rally neighbouring
tribes and thereby convince their leaders that resistance was useless. Force had to
be used after peaceful persuasion had failed.

The expedition against Tabūk, on the borders of the Byzantine empire, may
be the only case of an offensive operation undertaken by the Muslims. This
expedition was not designed to counter an imminent threat after the conquest
of Mecca and the submission of Thaqīf in Hunayn. Subsequent generations of
Muslims saw this expedition as an illustration of the duty of Muslims to impose
Islam beyond the boundaries of the Hejaz and the Arabian Peninsula. It is to
be noted, however, that this expedition was peaceful and bloodless, designed to
test the faith of recent converts to Islam and instil cohesion in their ranks, which
included Bedouins from around Medina and recent converts. Facing them were
hesitant and disaffected elements called "hypocrites" by the Qur'an. The expedition took place during the hot season and the episode known as the construction
of the "al Darar" mosque which seems to have been intended to rival that of the
Prophet. All these elements indicate that booty and plunder were not the main
reasons behind the expedition. Nor was it to direct attention toward an external
enemy as happened during the conquests under the second and third caliphs.[18]

Some may consider certain actions of the Prophet blameworthy or cruel,
as in the case of the treatment meted out to the Jews when their interests and
those of the Muslims diverged. Religious preaching has to take into account
the dynamics that govern a society if it wishes to exist within a given historical setting. A balance of power between different centres of power is one such
dynamic: division and disorder emanating from within a community or threat-
ening it from the outside cannot be tolerated. Critics should ask themselves if
any monotheist religion has spread in a peaceful manner. Would the preaching
of Muhammad have enjoyed any success among Arabs and non-Arabs had
it remained limited to a beleaguered minority of a few hundred souls threat-

ened by the Quraysh, who were determined to extirpate them by all possible means? The Jews were deliberately trying to sow dissension and division in Muslim ranks, defending their own religion and fearful of being marginalised or absorbed into the new religion which was taking shape. Violence is not, therefore, indispensable to Islam but rather was imposed by the historical context in which Islam developed. Any interpretation of verses concerning armed conflict which isolates them from their context flies in the face of historical reality.[19]

As for the role of leadership exercised by the Prophet in Medina, many Muslims believe that this was in the context of what is described, not without exaggeration, as an "Islamic state". In reality the Prophet did not adopt any of the titles befitting a position of leadership in such a "state". The title of king was not used, nor that of prince or any other such titles current among Arabs and non-Arabs at that time. A state, of whatever kind, needs a basic structure, whereas the Prophet had no currency, no ministries, officials, or permanent governors. All he did was appoint certain individuals for a particular task, such as carrying out the duties of *qādi* in a particular area or commanding an armed expedition. For the rest, his moral authority alone was a rallying point for the Muslim community. The main difference between the Prophet and other figures of authority would be that their influence was limited to their tribe or clan, whereas the Prophet's influence went beyond, and took precedence over, tribal allegiances without completely suppressing them. The authority of tribal chiefs was also based on their reputation and their possession of qualities, such as valour, manliness, courage and generosity required by their position in society. The Prophet relied on a religious legitimacy of which tribal chiefs did not dispose. In this sense his authority was not of a kind which could be bequeathed or applied as a criterion for a successor's authority: the authority of the Prophet ceased with his death and the transmission of his message.[20]

The debate about the Prophet's role in the Medinan period and the religious or political nature of his authority should have come to an end in 1344/1925 with the clarifications provided by Ali Abdelraziq in his famous book, *Islām wa Usūl al-hukm* (*Islam and the Foundations of Governance*), which clarified a number of points. One might also consider the variety of governments under which Muslims have lived since Ataturk's abolition of the Ottoman Caliphate in 1343/1924, a change that has not affected the way in which Muslims practise their religion. The dead weight of tradition remained unchanged, while the transition has been difficult from a traditional empire using religion to buttress its legitimacy to a modern nation state. Such a state is founded on the free election by citizens of their leaders and on the primacy of the will of the people as expressed in laws passed by representative assemblies. Law-making, executive and judicial powers are separated and all citizens are considered equal in rights and duties regardless of sex, belief, or other considerations.

What principles of morals and conduct are to be found in the sūras of the Qur'an revealed in the Medinan period? And what of the corpus of legislation drawn up by the *fuqahā'* in the second/eighth century derived from the words and deeds of the Prophet, considered by the *fuqahā'* as divine, binding law? It goes without saying that the Prophet had a daily teaching mission to those who had emigrated with him and to his Medinan allies (*Ansār*), working to change elements of traditional mentality and behaviour incompatible with Islamic values which rejected clan loyalty and tribalism, and were based on the common practice of pardon and forgiveness. The Prophet gave a constant example of upright behaviour and righteousness, while having a realistic attitude toward human nature and the character of his Companions, which oscillated between gentleness and violence, stubbornness, jealousy and the love of worldly pleasures. In the Prophet they had a "good example" to use the Qur'anic expression.[21] In his directives, orders and interdictions the horizon of the world to come was continually present, giving the ultimate meaning to human actions and inner aspirations. In other words, the Prophet was not so much interested in detailed social rules and regulations as he was in knowing if they could conform or not to the values he preached, such as pardon, generosity, an inner readiness for judgment and the world to come. He, therefore, recognised and perpetuated existing customs which did not run counter to Islamic principles, while insisting on individual responsibility for good or evil deeds. It is not the case that the directives of the Medinan period reduced in any way this dimension of personal responsibility destined to be progressively effaced in Muslim society after the death of the Prophet. Muhammad, as divine revelation repeats time and again, was sent by God in the same way as the other prophets. The message which he preached is the same as that of the prophets: that people may act justly. His task is to remind, to bear witness, to announce a message and call for vigilance: he is not a sovereign or guardian; he has not to force anyone to believe: "Each person is responsible for what they have acquired" and "do not bear what is the responsibility of another".[22]

In the light of these elements, one can understand the Qur'anic command to obey God and the Prophet and, in the same way, the Qur'an's instructions about the division of booty: "Whatever the Apostle gives you take; and whatever he forbids you, give over" (Sūra 59:7).[23] Whether it is a question of the most basic rules of behaviour – greeting, asking for permission to come in, entering a house, buying and selling, mortgages and debt, managing the property of orphans, dealing with the Jews and Christians or "People of the Book" (*Ahl al kitāb*), unbelievers, hypocrites, marriage, divorce, adultery, inheritances – or other matters confronting the Prophet while he was guiding the nascent Islamic community, there were two governing principles: on the one hand, attention to local conditions; and, on the other hand, encouraging the best possible code of conduct. This is the permanent defining characteristic of divine revelation and the actions of the Prophet. No violence or duress was employed. No Muslims were forced to go against their convictions. Nor did the Prophet impose decisions using the threat of harsh consequences in case of non-compliance. Self-appointed religious authorities have sacrificed truth and loyalty on the altar of external uniformity.

Does this contradict the instructions of the Qur'an which made the Prophet an arbitrator in disputes arising between Muslims? Far from it: recourse to an arbitrator in the case of disputes was a widespread practice among Arab tribes in the absence of a central government appointing judges. The parties involved in the dispute agreed beforehand to accept the verdict of the judge accepted by both parties. In a break with the past, the Prophet was not appointed as a judge because of prevailing tradition but due to his religious authority and moral leadership which made him superior to judges "whom one consults in their home", as the Arab proverb has it. It is natural that his authority should derive its legitimacy from a source unavailable to anyone else, that it should be the decision of God at a precise moment, so that Muslims could be educated according to Islamic values and morals, with justice and equality among believers superseding values weighted in favour of the rich and powerful at the expense of the weak and the poor. It is no mean task to change values and morals, especially in nomadic or quasi-nomadic societies which have deep-rooted traditions and customs, and where following tradition is the dominant trend. Without going into details about the solutions adopted by the Prophet in particular situations, it was in order to effect such a change that the Prophet carried out his mission.

The thrust of this research thus far leads inevitably to a radical overhaul of a central article of faith grounded in Islamic consciousness since the second/

ninth century. One has to recognise that what is essential is not the particular, historical reason for the existence of a given text or the general meaning of the words of the text; one has to transcend such considerations and examine the aim and intention of the text. There is room in this quest for a variety of interpretations, in the same way that people's needs are different, according to where and when and within which cultural milieu they live. There is also room for evolution, if a believer considers that the message of Muhammad is a matter of concern in the here and now of the present moment, without being obliged to interpret the message of the Prophet in the same way as his first/seventh-century contemporaries or successive generations of Muslims did. Present-day knowledge of traditional interpretations is in general second-hand and sketchy. It is as though Muslims, following blindly their scholars and leaders of legal schools and sects, have fallen into the same trap as the People of the Book before them, and worshipped false gods, a practice denounced by the Qur'an. Muslims have forgotten the flexibility which characterised the Prophet's teaching and conduct, turning them into examples to be memorised mechanically rather than pondered over.

It is instructive to compare, for example, the attitude of the Prophet to those drinking wine (he went no further than chastisement with the fringe of a item of clothing, a palm frond or a sandal) with that of Umār ibn al Khattāb and Ali ibn abī Tālib, who decreed that flogging should be the punishment.[24] The majority of the *fuqahā'* considered wine imbibing to be a grave infraction requiring the application of the same sanction. This is simply one example of the drift away from the path opened up by the preaching of the Prophet. Another comparison would be with the attitude of the Prophet toward a man who infringed the rule of Ramadhan by having sexual relations with his wife during the period of the Ramadhan fast. The Prophet requested that he make amends by making a charitable donation. As the man was poor the Prophet collected the sum due from his Companions.[25] However, the same man considered that he was more entitled to the donation and made off with it. Books of *fiqh* are full of references to *kaffārāt* (reparations) and attempts to go into painstaking detail about fasting regulations. One begins to grasp the basic difference between the conduct of the Prophet, based on tolerance, flexibility and understanding and the rigid attitude which Muslim scholars tried to impose.

To the above examples can be added the Qur'an's insistence that women should not be deprived of their share of the inheritance, in stark contrast to the imāms of legal schools and their successors who, right up until the present day, have considered the verses setting out this principle as a practical, obligatory and definitive solution to the question. In reality they are more akin to an initial, somewhat spontaneous reaction to the question which cannot, along with other verses relating to inheritance, be applied without recourse to arbitrary means or what scholars call "reductions". The same is true of polygamy, mentioned once by the Qur'an at the beginning of the Sūra al-Nisā' with a condition attached to it, namely that orphans be treated justly and equitably. The verse 129 of the same sūra states that this is impossible despite efforts in this direction. The same text authorises the taking of slaves as concubines, meaning that a free man can legitimately have sex with concubines of his choosing. The Qur'an was merely recognising what was current practice at the time in the Arabian peninsula and in numerous traditional societies. Certain elements, such as physical chastisement, are unacceptable today, although the Qur'an calls for spouses to be well treated and for exploitation and injustice to be avoided.

Muslims subsequently adopted attitudes to women which were far removed from, and even in outright contradiction to, this generally progressive outlook. This means that today there is an urgent need to carry out a comprehensive revision of the view that men and women exist in the context of a hierarchy and not as different and complementary. Women are seen as instruments for procuring pleasure for men. Women are not perceived as persons having the same rights and responsibilities as men. Demoted to an inferior position, women's freedoms are limited, and they are confined to the roles of housewife and mother with the obligation to wear a veil. It is certain that women in Muslim societies are gaining recognition of rights of which they were deprived in the past, an important change in societies which are moving away from traditional lifestyles into a phase of industrialisation and integration in today's global economy. This does not mean rejecting Islamic values, although it may mean the progressive abandonment of certain precepts for reasons of realism and practicality. Opposition will come from those groups in society in whose interest it is that women remain subservient, imagining at the same time that they are somehow more faithful than others to the teachings of their religion.[26]

In the context of discussion of the family, it is necessary to address the question of adultery and its sanction. The Qur'an decreed flogging, not stoning to death.[27] The *fuqahā'* later decided on the latter penalty on the basis of an abrogated verse which retains its legal validity. A precedent set by the Prophet exists, although its authenticity is dubious. Flogging is prescribed by the Qur'an, and it is the most severe sanction apart from that reserved for *qadhf*, accusing a woman of adultery without the four necessary witnesses.[28] One hundred strokes are prescribed in the case of adultery, to be reduced by half when slaves were the guilty party, eighty in the case of *qadhf*.[29]

This sanction was intended to prevent the spread of adultery and the consequent confusion over lineage and descendants in a society which attached great importance, as did all nomadic societies, to the purity of lineages. Men did not need to have sexual relations unlawfully, since they could have more than one wife and possess an unlimited number of concubines. The possibility also existed of a temporary marriage (*zawāj al mutaʾa* or "marriage of pleasure") which has been abolished by the Sunnis, although not by the Shiʿa: it still exists in Iran, to the advantage of religious functionaries in particular.[30] Islamic societies throughout history have, however, still not digested the novel principle of equality between men and women, nor have they been rigorous in applying the strict conditions required for the application of the punishment for adultery.[31] The requirement that there be four witnesses makes it virtually impossible to apply the sanction.

One might also consider the question of divorced or widowed women and the "waiting period". The reason for this practice is to make sure that the woman is not pregnant. This delay is obligatory for women while men can marry without delay. Today tried, tested and straightforward scientific means exist which show whether or not a woman is pregnant. Is it really necessary to wilfully ignore innovations in the field of science and physiology which have shed light on domains which remained obscure at the time of the Prophet? Does one have to cling to a literal interpretation of the sacred texts without trying to understand their finality in the light of scientific progress? These, and similar questions, should give food for thought to those who preach reconciliation between reason and tradition. Tradition always entails interpretation and the best interpretation is that which preserves the spirit of the text without turning it into something static and unchanging.

Sexuality is a delicate subject in all societies, ancient and modern, one which religions, systems of morality and laws try to regulate. Account must be taken, however, of the changes in the relations between men and women.[32] The place occupied by myth and superstition in these relations has been reduced, while women for the first time in history can exercise control over their own bodies and pregnancy has become a voluntary choice. Sanctions, whether they concern usury, theft, or other questions, are not simply to be applied out of blind obedience to unchanging divine commands unconnected to any particular time or place. These have been imposed by social and ethical imperatives which today are no longer relevant. They can be modified, influenced as they are by changing factors, social, economic or political in nature.

5

The Seal of Prophecy

From these and similar examples one can deduce that the religious message of Muhammad had one significant distinguishing feature. This message belonged to what Muhammad Iqbal called "the ancient world", not merely, as Iqbal pointed out, because of its source, but also because his message included a number of elements rooted in the society of the time. However, as Iqbal says, "insofar as the spirit of his revelation is concerned, he belongs to the modern world".[1] The need for an invisible source of power, the presence of images drawn from mythology, for rites uniformly accomplished with no room for variation among adherents of the religion,[2] the consecration of a number of social values and practices: all of this reflects a way of looking at the world which is not fundamentally different from that of the Arabs and peoples everywhere over many centuries. It is impossible to impose this traditional way of looking at the world on those who have experienced transformations which have radically affected human consciousness as well as the material dimensions of existence. Human history does not stand still nor is its course reversed, although human needs are universal: food; clothing; sexual relations; shelter; self-expression; life in a community; a sense of security both physically and emotionally; and, above all, a need to give life and destiny some kind of meaning. These needs can be met in a simple, unsophisticated way or in a refined and complex way in the modern world.

One question which needs to be answered, however the question is framed, would be the following: did the message of Muhammad aim at halting human development at a particular stage which would not be surpassed? Did the Prophet try to confer an aura of absolutism to his instructions and the guidance he gave? Or, on the contrary, did he strive to broaden people's horizons and give them complete responsibility for the way that worship should be conducted and daily life organised? In doing this they would be free to follow the dictates of their conscience. The second facet of Muhammad's message noted by Muhammad Iqbal should be reexamined. It is one that has tended to languish in obscurity and whose innovative capacity has been neglected. Muslims have been unused to exploring this hitherto hidden facet of Islam, uncovering its secrets and their meaning. Most Muslims, one may even venture to say, were unaware of its existence. This was not through negligence or inability on their part but simply because the confines of the culture and the context in which they lived imposed certain models of thought and conduct.

Iqbal, in a remark that is concise yet charged with meaning, expressed all of this with unrivalled eloquence and insight when he said: "In Islam, prophecy reached its perfection in discovering the need for its own abolition. This involves the keen perception that life cannot be forever kept in drawing strings; that in order to reach full self-consciousness man must be thrown back on his own resources."[3] Yet, how can Iqbal or anyone else determine that "in Islam, prophecy reached its perfection in discovering the need for its own abolition" and then consider the necessity of abolition as the highest degree of prophetic perfection? Is this not imposing on Islam ideas that are foreign to it? The answer depends on how the term "seal of prophecy" is understood.[4] Does it simply mean that Muhammad is the last of the prophets?

Logically there seem to be only two ways of interpreting the term "seal" of the prophecy. The first possibility that comes to mind, one that is widely circulated in Islamic texts, and with which the majority of Muslims agree, imagining that it is the only possibility, would be that line of prophets was closed from the inside, as it were, and that the last prophet concludes this line while remaining a part of it. He is necessarily an integral part of this line that he concludes, and cannot depart from it or transcend it in any way. He can be compared with someone who locks a door as he enters a house and remains confined inside. The term of "seal" in this sense indicates merely a chronological order and that Muhammad comes at the end of a series of prophets, the last of the long line beginning with Adam and ending with Muhammad. If this prophetic structure contained any common elements between Muhammad and his predecessors, then Muhammad would have to adopt those elements in their entirety, applying to himself what applied to them down to the last detail, as there was no difference between their prophetic messages and his.

If the prophets before him were sent only to their own peoples, Muhammad was, therefore, primarily the prophet of the Arabs. If other prophets were kings, such as David and Solomon, Muhammad would be invested with the trappings of a king, a holder of political authority and the founder of a state. Where other prophets were legislators, such as Moses, Muhammad introduced legislation similar to their legislation or superior to it. As all the prophets worked miracles – Moses parting the waters with his staff, Jesus speaking while still in the cradle or bringing the dead to life – Muhammad was bound to do the same kind of physical miracles: multiplying quantities of food; causing water to gush forth; curing the sick, being endowed with exceptional sexual potency; and so on.[5] In other words, Muhammad had to be like them in everything they did, while surpassing them in terms of the mission he accomplished and in the means he employed. The only difference was that Muhammad was the last of the prophets.[6]

This understanding of prophecy is hardly surprising since people generally tend to evaluate what is new and unexpected in terms of what is familiar and are rarely attentive to what is new. In other words, they can reflect only on the basis of what exists and what resonates within them. Something that is beyond the frontiers of thought at a particular moment and what is inconceivable to someone living at a particular period may nevertheless be present, one may say, in a latent or potential form. Its meaning remains hidden beneath dense layers of interpretation and understanding which have diverted it from its original aims and long-term aspirations. Its power remains latent, awaiting the appropriate moment and the most suitable setting and people. At that point it emerges into view, bursting onto the scene in such a way that people are astonished that it had languished in obscurity for so long without attracting attention and being taken up.

Consider, for example, how Muslims until recently viewed the holder of political authority, whatever his title: caliph; king; *amīr*; or sultan; he "over whom there is no higher power", to use the expression of Ibn Khaldoun. He was not held to account for what he did and obedience was owed to him even though he might be an oppressor. One may also consider the duty of the ruler (about which there is general agreement) to consult "citizens", traditionally considered his "subjects". Islamic thought from the time of the caliph Abu Bakr in the first/seventh century up until the nineteenth century went no further than the position outlined by al-Māwardi in the fifth/twelfth century in *The Statutes of Government* (*al-ahkām as-sultāniyya*) when he recognises that investiture should be carried out, when the ruler's office is vacant, by those who "have the power to bind and release". No one envisaged consultation in other circumstances or while the ruler exercised his power.[7]

Today many Muslims (including some of the leaders of Islamist movements) do not refuse democracy on the grounds that it is "un-Islamic"; on the contrary, they see in the two Qur'anic verses mentioning consultation a reliable source justifying consultation and even democracy.[8] They would not have interpreted the Qur'an in this way had not modern sensibility come to firmly reject absolute government, striving to limit absolute government and to keep them under formal supervision. This is just one way in which concepts which may have been unknown to Muslims in the past are no less legitimate than those of which they approved. When favourable circumstances allow latent insights to emerge, new ideas can replace older concepts without believers feeling that they are guilty of reckless innovation and transgression.

The second possibility is to understand the term "seal of prophecy" as being a closure of the prophetic line from the outside, as it were. Seen in these terms the seal of prophecy is one that puts a definitive end to the human need to rely on an external source of knowledge and norm for conduct. It, therefore, announces the opening of a new era in human history, in which humans, having reached maturity, no longer require a guide on whom to rely in every aspect of existence no matter how trifling. The task of the Prophet of Islam is, therefore, to guide people to a new sense of responsibility and acceptance of the results of their own choices. The Prophet can, therefore, be compared with someone closing the door of a house, in this case the house of all the prophets, and closing it from the outside. The Prophet was, therefore, no longer a prisoner inside the house and was quite free. He had announced that people were free to live in houses constructed by their own efforts and guided by their reason and intelligence, as well as the interests of each individual and society. The Prophet is sent as a true witness, bearing good tidings and warning "O Prophet, we have sent thee as a witness, and good tidings to bear, and warning" and by his words and deeds is a "good example", to use the Qur'anic expression.[9] He gave an example of justice, charity, compassion, goodness and upright conduct generally adapted to the circumstances in which he lived. He had not determined once and for all what people should do and not do, in all circumstances and all situations. Had he done this he would have reinforced the spirit of conformism that he had come in order to oppose, substituting one tradition with another, albeit superior to what already existed.

The message of liberation brought by Islam is not compatible with the orientation taken by Islamic thought, one that emphasised external compliance with the practices of the Prophet. The great Sufi thinkers constitute a possible exception. This imitation turned into the adoption of a rigid legal shell which was imposed on believers.[10] True freedom comes only through understanding the reasons and experiences which shaped the practice of the Prophet and led him to adopt particular courses of action. One of the basic functions of religion is to reduce the *angst* that individuals experience, although if this entails a denial of human freedom people will end up living in a state similar to that of animals in hibernation in an extremely cold habitat: their activity is reduced to the basic functions which assure their survival. If individuals are prevented from acting, they merely drift into passivity and what is best in them withers away: imagination; creativity; courage in the face of oppression; an independent conscience, everything, in short, that represents an unfettered personality with a unique place in the world.

It is true that the human quest for truth resembles the progress of a blind person who perceives the world by relying on senses other than sight, while religion, Islam in the present case, is the language which enables him or her to fathom the enigmas of human life. Nothing, though, can replace a personal quest for values which are worth striving for alongside other like-minded individuals, certainly not formal adhesion to an inherited form of religiosity, nor a programme of practice and prescriptions imposed by an institution, nor undiscriminating and slavish imitation of a role model (were it the Prophet himself let alone sundry imāms and other religious figures) in the minutiae of daily life, such as what to wear. Muhammad b. 'Abdallah thus concluded, or "put a seal" on the line of the prophets, ending the practices of repetition and learning by rote, opening the way toward a future that people will build together in a spirit of freedom, responsibility and solidarity. He laid down the solid foundation for a truly universal code of ethics, and his role as a Prophet was no longer one of offering ready-made patterns of behaviour for Muslims to apply in a mechanical fashion.

One can imagine the chorus of disapproval that these ideas will provoke. Can the whole Muslim community have reached a consensus built on errors? What will remain of Islam if Muslims turn away from the path followed hitherto? Some of this doom-mongering is fuelled by a desire to preserve material or spiritual interests and to perpetuate the status quo despite the crisis of traditional religious practice in modern society. The weight of the past and of tradition should also be set aside. Who gave these self-appointed spokesmen the right to speak in the name of the "real" Islam? Since when has the work of scholars been an expression of what is in the heart of Muslims? Do they share in God's knowledge of people's innermost thoughts? How do these spokesmen know that one day Muslims will not develop a deeper understanding of their faith than that which has prevailed for fourteen centuries, a period which is short when seen in the context of the broad sweep of human history? Are people not called upon to explore the world and examine it, created as it is by God? When they seriously take up this invitation they discover that God addresses them through the "symphony of creation" in which they participate inasmuch as they are creatures capable, as no others are, of enriching the created world by the spontaneous fruits of their imagination and the disciplined processes of their intelligence. No one can replace them in this role; it is they alone who can add their voices to the hymn of creation that surrounds them if they are attentive to their deepest thoughts and the song of creation, be it audible or silent. Nothing can stand in the way of their search for the best and most suitable ways of organising their lives and attaining happiness. Muslims should be proud that the message of the Prophet exhorts them to do this, calling on them to react to events and not regulate their lives according to the practice of their forebears, to explore human existence in all its richness and not simply repeat slogans, and to bring up the next generation to think for themselves and not cling mulishly to a list of formulas learnt by heart.

Roman Catholic theologians, in particular since the Second Vatican Council (1962–5), have tended to maintain that the Church has retreated from some of its previous positions (which were in some cases erroneous) because of a deeper understanding of the deposit of faith rather than because of a desire to disavow its own history, a desire which would deal a fatal blow to the dogma of infallibility.[11] Islam does not recognise (fortunately, in our opinion) the principle of a clerical class, nor is it a matter of disquiet that Muslims may have made mistakes. None the less, a particular interpretation or a way of understanding adopted by one particular or several generations, although valid in a particular cultural or historical context, may need to be superseded or abandoned in a different context. This is equally true of Shī'ite and Sunni thought, for both address Muslims in a schoolmasterly tone. Shī'ism requires a second "cycle", the cycle of holiness (*walāya*), which perpetuates the process of revelation through the imām and the saints; their attributions have changed but their prophetic function remains. Sunnism retains only the most superficial understanding of the term "seal of prophecy", clinging to a literal interpretation of the text and prescribing obedience to edicts based on the deductions of religious scholars of the second/eighth century, as if contemporary Muslims are incapable of making their own deductions.[12] In both cases there is a clear deviation from what we believe God intended by ending the prophetic line. Sunnism and Shī'ism keep individual believers in a state of subordination to religious leaders, whatever the names or titles they may be given. They instil a fear of both the responsibility brought by the message of Muhammad and the radical equality of rights and duties for all Muslims.

For all these reasons we can state unhesitatingly that the message of Islam took into account the needs of its time. The essence of the message was far in advance of its time and it far outstripped the thoughts and aspirations of Muhammad's contemporaries. The message was rich in possibilities and perspectives, although Muslims were open only to those closest to the prevailing mentality. They cannot be blamed for the results of their efforts of interpretation and deduction: those who should be criticised are those who persist in adhering to traditional positions and do not give sufficient weight to the need of people today for spiritual sustenance which goes beyond automatic obedience and literal application of orders and prohibitions. They do not perceive the important evolution that has taken place in what is known as "the public sphere",[13] moving from a situation in which everyone had a more or less equal chance of deriving knowledge from a few uniform sources and only simple questions were debated to one unprecedented in history where sources of knowledge are well-nigh limitless. This is due to the spread of education across a broad sector of society, the diffusion of books, magazines and newspapers and the rapid transmission (rendered instantaneous by the Internet) of audio-visual information across the world.

Part Two

The Message in History

Introduction

People do not discover truth, they construct it, as they construct their history.

(P. Veyne)

This part will not be concerned with the detail of historical events, despite the need for a critical examination of the history of the Muslim community after the death of the Prophet, during the time of the rightly-guided caliphs,[1] and the subsequent Umayyad period (41/661–126/744).[2] It was only towards the middle of the second/eighth century that the period after the death of the Prophet began to be documented. This documentation was incomplete and influenced by the partisan rivalries of the different factions involved. Some Muslims accepted the official version of events, others contested it, while yet others gave tacit approval. Underlying these events is a question which this part aims to answer: given the nature of the message of Muhammad, why did the first Muslims not put this message into practice? Why did the Companions, the Followers,[3] and those who came after them adopt solutions which seem unsatisfactory, and even spurious?

The divergence between the aims of Muhammad's preaching and its historical form is not something that should cause surprise. This divergence is a feature of philosophical and religious movements. This is what happened in the case of Protestantism, which developed alongside modernity, leading to results which were far from conforming to the vision of the founding fathers of Protestantism, and in some cases, in contradiction to it.[4] The same could be said of Marxism as applied in the former Soviet Union. It is not a question of analysing the intentions of the first Muslims, who acted with a clear conscience, believing that they were acting in complete fidelity to the new religion and its demands. They acted almost on impulse, without a theoretical framework to govern their conduct which only became a reference for the Muslim community long after this first generation of believers had left the scene.

The passage of time has rendered futile any attempt to unearth the motivation of that generation or that of any faction among them. It can be stated with some certainty that the aura of sinless perfection with which they have been surrounded does not reflect historical reality. This legend was grounded in the need of the political establishment for legitimacy, a need shared by the religious scholars or 'ulamā'. History abounds with examples (which it is pointless to enumerate) of the first believers' involvement in violent conflicts, as they rivalled one another in accumulating wealth and enjoying worldly pleasures: womanising; owning concubines and slaves; revelling in palaces, clothes and luxury.[5] Such conduct was natural and unsurprising, as values which challenge prevailing customs take time to become established and adopted, before superseding traditional values. Their assimilation is a gradual process and depends on prevailing conditions within society.

1

The Prophet's Successors

There were a number of possible scenarios for the transitional period after the Prophet's death which saw the message of Muhammad begin to take on a socio-political dimension.

(1) A return to the status quo prevailing in the Hejaz before Muhammad. This was inconceivable in the light of the new situation created by the preaching of the Prophet in the Hejaz and in the Arabian peninsula, with the interpersonal and collective solidarities created by Islam transcending traditional tribal structures. The initial signs of social fragmentation had already appeared before the beginning of Muhammad's preaching, accompanied by a vague yet powerful yearning for change. In the light of these factors, it was inevitable that some kind of centralised decision-making process should begin to take form. The tribe of the Quraysh, because of its prestige among the Arabs, its illustrious history and its economic power had a strong chance of playing a central political role after the Prophet's death. Tribal loyalties may also explain the revolt known as the *ridda* (apostasy) which broke out among tribes outside the Hejaz at the time of Abū Bakr. This movement was an expression of an obsolescent tribal solidarity which had begun to disintegrate. Even if Muhammad and the Muslim community had not decisively confronted the *ridda*, it was doomed to fail.

(2) Another possible outcome could have been the adoption (for their own ends) of the preaching of the Prophet by the rich and powerful members of the Quraysh, although their initial resistance rendered this unlikely. The subsequent course of events demonstrates that the Ummayads adopted this course of action once the passage of time had drawn a veil over their past record. At the same time,

the vast Islamic empire, composed of a multitude of races and interest groups, needed Umayyad skills in organisation and intrigue, as well as their economic resources and adeptness in political manoeuvre.

(3) Another eventuality was a revised version of the *Sahīfa* Agreement. This was an agreement of a non-religious character between the emigrants from Mecca (*muhājirūn*) and the inhabitants of Medina (Yathrib), Aws, Khazradj and the Jews.[1] The weak position of the Muslim community prior to the expulsion of the Jews, the conquest of Mecca and the ensuing conversion to Islam of the peninsular tribes made such an agreement necessary. Changing circumstances removed the justification for such an agreement: as the community's position had gone from one of weakness to strength, while Islamic principles had been applied in numerous areas and religious affiliation had become the basis of social cohesion.

(4) The events surrounding the *Sahīfa* incident[2] show that internal conflict could have divided the Muslim community. The *Muhājirūn* considered that the Quraysh were most qualified to exercise authority following the Prophet's death, while the *Ansār*[3] saw this as an attempt to marginalise them. Setting out their position, 'Umar said: "And lo, they are trying to cut us off from our origin and wrest authority from us". Their speaker continuing, replied: "We are God's Helpers and the squadron of Islam; you, *Muhājirūn*, are a family of ours and a company of your people has come to settle." All the *Ansār* would accept was a sharing of power: "Let us have one ruler, and you another, Quraysh."[4] 'Umar provoked surprise by hastening to swear allegiance to Abū Bakr, exploiting the rivalry between Aws and Khazradj. Haunted by the spectre of a fratricidal struggle for power, he declared:

> We feared that if we left the assembly without having sworn allegiance to a Caliph, they would have chosen one of those present after we had left. We would have had to accept their choice even if we disapproved of it, or oppose them, which would have been a disaster.[5]

(5) Yet another possibility would have been to entrust the *Ahl al Bait* ("People of the House") in the form of 'Ali or 'Abbās with the control of affairs. This would have meant bringing together symbolic authority (being related to the Prophet) and temporal authority, which was the object of contention. 'Ali's personality may have played a part in excluding him, although it seems that there was also something of a reluctance to accept the principle of accumulating

different types of authority in the hands of one person. Power concentrated in this way, exercised for good or ill, would have been difficult to resist. The Arabs were unfamiliar with such practices and were unwilling to accept them even if the Shīʿa subsequently saw the convergence of symbolic and temporal authority as representing the highest degree of legality.

(6) The last option, the one that came to pass, was adopted because of the disadvantages associated with the other possible outcomes. Abū Bakr was designated as successor to the Prophet. The factors of age, experience and personal charisma played an important role in his nomination as tribal tradition demanded. The prestige that he enjoyed among the Muslims made it difficult for any rival faction to oppose him. As a member of the council of the Quraysh, the earliest form of a state institution, he was approved by the rich members of this tribe. Under his guidance, events during the *ridda* followed the traditional pattern in the peninsula: the Quraysh's prestige continued to grow and refractory tribes were brought into its sphere of influence.

Two remarks should be made at this point: first, that religious considerations were either completely absent or of secondary importance in the designation of Abū Bakr to succeed the Prophet. Claims that he was the preferred candidate because he was the first convert to Islam or because he led the community in prayer while the Prophet was ill were made *a posteriori* in order to confer legitimacy on this choice. Textual authority for the caliphate of Abū Bakr only appeared in certain Sunni circles at a later period as a reaction to Shīʿite claims that ʿAli was the rightful imām. The choice of a person to lead the community was a purely practical one, a necessity caused by the power vacuum after the death of the Prophet, who had exercised power without facing any opposition. It was also the application of a universal social law, namely that human collectivities, whatever their size, need a figure of authority who will represent them. If such a figure does not exist, anarchy will prevail and the organisation necessary to perpetuate the life of the collectivity will be gravely damaged.[6] Islam developed in an environment in which the state was absent, which explains why religion and state converged from the time of Abū Bakr onwards. It became impossible to imagine the continued existence of Islam without it enjoying the protection of the state. This was at the expense of the vitality of the message and its capacity to develop.

The second point to be made would be that the designation of Abū Bakr to this post, along with that of later caliphs, kings, amīrs and sultans was of no concern to the overwhelming majority of Muslims.[7] The only people concerned were leaders and those who had some influence over them, to whom the literature of the governmental statutes (*al-ahkām al-sultāniyya*) gave the name of "those who have the power to bind and loose". Power could not be exercised by the governor except with their support or approval, or at least with their acceptance of his authority. This means that soon after the Prophet's death there was a drift away from a spirit of equality between Muslims. There was a resurgence of traditional values at the expense of the revolutionary values proclaimed by the new religion. In other words, the institution of a democratic electoral system in today's sense of the term was inconceivable to Muslims at that time. Democracy is the fruit of an evolution which has taken humankind two or three centuries and does not have a direct link with religion. Within religion there is a factor of alienation and at the same time religion bears the seeds of liberation from alienation: this potential remains latent until the conditions are ripe for it to take on a specific form within human history. Consultation of the people was limited to a very small number of individuals, before dwindling away completely and being replaced by an hereditary system and the nomination of successors. None of this was due to Islam. The role of religion is to confer legitimacy on existing or projected structures of power. Subjective religious consciousness present within each believer is the deciding factor in determining whether or not a particular system of government conforms to the principles of the message of the Prophet. It is evident that individual sensitivities change and evolve and are very different in the twenty-first century from what they were in the seventh century CE.

Various theoretical scenarios existed which could have filled the vacuum caused by the death of Muhammad, although the chances of their coming to pass varied greatly. The final turn of events did not necessarily conform most closely to the logic of the Prophet's message: in the end prevailing historical circumstances determined which scenario came to pass. Two important areas of social life, slavery and women in society, were influenced by the prevailing context in such a way that the spirit of the of the Prophet's message was set aside. They have been grouped together, as they lie at the heart of an eminent principle which is Qur'anic as well as human, that of personal dignity.

The first area is that of slavery, a phenomenon which is of merely historical interest today, although one may still wonder why Muslims enslaved their fellow men and women while remaining deaf to the message of revelation. The Qur'an emphasised the pre-eminent position that God has assigned to humankind as a whole and also multiplied the occasions on which they could be freed: the practical result of this would be to put an end to the practice of slavery. It is noteworthy that the Qur'an does not mention a single case or set of circumstances in time of war or in peace which could lead to one individual enslaving other humans. The conquests (*futūhāt*) quickly became a means of acquiring fresh provender, with Arab masters exploiting male slaves for their own gain in various forms of forced labour while female slaves were totally subjected to their master's whims and desires. Muslims seemed to forget the logic of the message of Islam and its aim, as well as its necessary gradualism and realism in not confronting directly existing interests. Their behaviour toward slaves was similar to that of non-Muslims, or the pre-Islamic inhabitants of Arabia, and sometimes worse. Worldly interest and greedy material considerations prevented a coherent interpretation of the Islamic message and Muslims lost the opportunity of being the first heralds of human rights in the broad, direct sense of the term, and the first to put them into practice among peoples for whom it was normal that not all people should be free. Jurists went no further than to enjoin slave owners to treat their slaves well, while making the same remarks with regard to animals.

The second area was that of women and their rights. Here again Muslims were no more innovative than other contemporary peoples. The inferiority of women was a firmly rooted belief in all ancient cultures, with the "second sex" being seen as associated with weakness, evil, an ally of Satan himself. Merely physiological phenomena, such as menstrual blood, were in the eyes of most people signs of female impurity during menstruation. A woman could not approach food intended for other people lest it become unfit for consumption; she would be placed apart in a place set aside for this.[8] Had not women been created from one of Adam's ribs? Had she not led him astray by persuading him to eat the fruit of the tree, an act which was the source of sin and precipitated the expulsion of Adam and Eve from Paradise? Muslims are well aware that the Qur'an says nothing about these two myths present in the Book of Genesis and, on the contrary, emphasises that people are created from a single vital source of life and that God created a partner for man that he might dwell with her. The Qur'an states equally clearly that Iblīs[9] was the source of temptation, not Eve, and that God pardoned Adam thus effacing the act of disobedience. Instead of meditating on all of this, the Muslims set about adopting elements of the Jewish legends or *isra'iliyyāt*[10] which reinforced preconceived ideas on women and interpreted the Qur'anic verses concerning women in an arbitrary way which abolished the essential differences between the preaching of Muhammad and the texts of the *Ahl al-Kitāb*.[11] They were, therefore, unable to attain the noble aims of the Qur'an and show how Islam was the basis of a system of values which broke with tradition and commonly held beliefs.

Even more regrettable was the way in which they conceived Islam through the prism, as it were, of their desires, fancies and selfish interests, which meant that Islam became synonymous with the oppression and degradation of women who were confined to their homes behind bunker-like walls, deprived (because of Islam) of their basic human rights such as education and employment. Islam is manipulated in order to shore up an uncertain religious and cultural identity which asserts itself by a deluded obligation placed on young girls to wear the veil.[12] Here, too, Muslims missed the opportunity of being the precursors in recognising men and women as equal. Where women have been able to obtain – with difficulty – certain of their legitimate rights, this has been against the will of men and without any cooperation on their part. This would not have been the case had they possessed a deep understanding of the message of Islam. What were the historical factors at the origin of this aberrant interpretation of Islam?

These factors are multiple and interconnected. It is difficult to isolate them from one another or to consider one more important than another. Some are of cultural origin, such as the residual pre-Islamic mentality among the Arabs or among Muslims belonging to other cultures and religions in the conquered territories. Those who embraced the new religion did not undergo a type of "brainwashing" but brought with them their way of looking at the world, together with their beliefs, sensitivities and values. In the light of all of these they came to understand the elements of Muhammad's preaching with which they came into contact, as well as the texts that they had discovered. As might be expected in such circumstances, they fell back on old frames of reference in order to understand what was novel and unfamiliar. This led to a certain number of concerns being projected onto Islam, as it were, which were foreign to it, and even contrary to its spirit and aims. On the other hand, the existing knowledge of nature, its laws, human beings and their inner life and aspirations, society and its norms conditioned the way in which the first generations of Muslims understood religious teachings. This understanding acquired a sacred character with the passage of time which it was difficult to cast off even when learning progressed and set aside obsolete views.

Other factors were political in character, connected with the need to conduct the affairs of the community in a given historical environment. As the tribal and clan system prevailed in the Arabian peninsula, it was not to be expected that the designation of the leaders of the Islamic community and their exercise of power should somehow inaugurate new and unfamiliar forms. This is why the first three caliphs, known as the *rāshidūn* or "rightly-guided ones",[13] and the first Umayyad rulers behaved like tribal or factional chiefs despite the extent of their suzerainty which extended over groups of people very different from those ruled by tribal chiefs in the Arabian peninsula and covered an infinitely greater area. Kinship played an important role in the code of tribal ethics, and remained significant under Islam, with non-Arabs being denied the rights and privileges enjoyed by the Arabs. Muslims of Arab origin appropriated for themselves the highest political and military ranks in the nascent empire while the non-Arabs (*mawāli*)[14] and foreign Muslims in general were excluded from them. The bitterness that this exclusion fuelled made them easy prey for power-hungry insurgent movements and led them, in reaction to their exclusion, to swell the ranks of the largely Persian *shu'ubiyya* movement.[15] Many of the *mawāli* sought to surpass the Arabs in fields which the latter considered with disdain: science in general, as well as religious and linguistic studies.

These political factors are also linked to the practical necessities of the construction of the state and the administrative apparatus, albeit rudimentary, on which it reposed. It was natural that these administrative structures reproduced those existing in pre-Islamic Mecca. That environment had offered an experience limited in scope and of little value in the context of a multicultural, multiethnic empire transcending the bounds of the tribal system with its uncomplicated components. Traditional structures of government had to be reinforced by drawing on the experience of neighbouring peoples in dealing with a civil service, money, taxes, land and its ownership. The running of the expanding empire necessitated the founding of a pensions office to compensate for the inability of memory alone to retain the names of those entitled to draw a pension and the amount each would receive. Then came other branches of the administration: army; post; chancellery; and the other services needed by a central authority.[16] As these structures were set up, Muslims did not feel that they had to observe religious precepts: it was a practical question, consisting, on the one hand, of adopting systems existing among states of the region, and, on the other hand, of inventing solutions which would preserve social stability. This appears very clearly in the case of statutes concerning conquered land, which varied from one locality to another. Another example would be the refusal of 'Umār to distribute the fertile land (*sawād*) of Iraq to those who had participated in their conquest. Human institutions require, as we have seen, legitimacy in the eyes of those who benefit from them as well in the eyes of those who submit to the authority of these institutions. No sooner had they been set up than a authoritative foundation was sought for them, which at that time was religious in nature. It is highly probable that the motivation for decisions taken at a political level was not so much religious as practical. Sometimes this meant following closely the principles of Muhammad's message, at other times it meant departing from them.

Economic factors also played a significant role in the deviant interpretations of the message of Islam at the hands of the first generation of Muslims as well as in the way the message was lived out in practical terms. With the exception of the principal traders in Mecca, the inhabitants of the peninsula, whether Bedouin or sedentary, led hard, austere lives because of the desert environment. They also experienced poverty and privation because of the lack of natural resources. Such was their situation in the pre-Islamic period, and this continued at the time of the Prophet and during the caliphate of Abū Bakr. Scarcely had 'Umar ibn al-Khattāb succeeded him than he realised in a moment of far-sighted genius that the best way to heal the antagonism between adherents of the new religion and the divisions caused by the civil war which had occupied his predecessor, Abū Bakr, was to direct the combatants' energies toward an external enemy. This was a classic solution applied in many similar circumstances, although in this case rapidity of execution and exploitation of the element of surprise meant that success was total even if the balance of force was tilted clearly in favour of the two great powers of the time, Persia and Byzantium. They did not anticipate that the Arabs would attack them, a people whom they had grown accustomed to consider as being fragmented and fractious. They had underestimated the profound transformation brought about by Islam, one that affected the mentality of the Arabs and led to shared religious faith superseding tribal solidarities.

The amazing speed and relative ease with which the conquests were carried out during the caliphate of 'Umar are almost without historical parallels: Byzantium lost control of Syria and Egypt, while the Persian empire in Iraq and Iran was swept away. In comparison with the short-lived conquest by Alexander the Great of vast swathes of the known world in the fourth century BCE, the Arab conquests had consequences which outlasted the caliphate of 'Umar and survived the transfer of power to his successors. A series of victories in North Africa brought the Arabs to the frontiers of Europe in the Iberian Peninsula and the south of what is now France, battle lines which were stable for about a century. Two aspects of these conquests are of particular interest in the context of this book and are discussed below.

First, by conquering countries which were rich in natural resources, arts and crafts, and where ancient civilisations had flourished, the Arabs had amassed booty which surpassed their expectations and even their wildest dreams, given the poor environment in which they lived and the impoverished state of the Arabian peninsula.[17] The direct result of this was the growth of a class of *nouveaux riches* belonging to the traditional Qurayshi governing class who had organised and led the conquests, as well as a number of the *Ansār* who had distinguished themselves at that time. Predictably, "treasures of gold and silver" were amassed, in contradiction to the message of the Qur'an.[18] The opposition voiced by Abū Dhurr al Ghifāri and others was to no avail. As Muslim believers, they were shocked by the amassing of wealth and the resulting harmful disparities between different classes of Muslims, with a minority possessing vast tracts of fertile land generating wealth for their owners who then flaunted it in marriages, rival building projects, fine clothes, armies of servants and livestock and sumptuous lifestyles in general. Abd er Rahmān ibn 'Awf, al-Zubayr ibn al-'Awāmm and Talha ibn 'Ubayd Allah[19] exemplified this trend, while the majority of Arabs and foreign converts to Islam experienced economic hardship and did not benefit from the booty accumulated during the conquests, or other consequences of the conquests: income; territory; estates; the extension of trading routes; as well as the benefits deriving from holding high office in the various provinces under the suzerainty of the caliph.

The effects of the conquest were not limited to the material sphere. They engendered an entrepreneurial mentality, one that calculated the relation between aims and means of achieving them, reinforcing tendencies already present in the mercantile mentality of Qurayshi notables in the pre-Islamic period. In the same way it buttressed relations based on obedience, factional loyalties and the submission of the weak to the strong, all of which flew in the face of the relations that Islam tried to install which were founded on justice and equality. Obedience can eventually turn into refusal and rebellion, and it is no surprise that the seeds of organised sedition and revolt which marked Islamic history from that early period of the conquests, producing their deadly fruit at the time of 'Uthmān's caliphate. Subsequent theories of law, theology and ethics were also influenced by all these developments, with the 'ulamā' willingly adopting Persian values and taking the emperors as models of conduct, as though there were no difference between imperial values and the message of Islam.[20] This system of subservience also had an effect on the education of the young in society, with the following generations growing up accustomed to complying with what others wanted, instead of cultivating within them mutual respect and equality. An ethical approach based on freedom and responsibility did not develop. This would have allowed them to respect the rules of society, while recognising that these could evolve by democratic means.[21]

The second significant aspect of the conquests is their legitimacy from the point of view of the logic of the message of the Prophet. Merely raising this may appear singular, as Muslims have been used to considering what befell their ancestors in the first century of Islam as a benediction which led them from the darkness into the light and guided them onto the road of righteousness after they had wandered astray. In the context of the present study, however, the question is not raised from this point of view. One may, however, wonder if the occupation of the conquered territories was a holy war (*jihād*) in the Qur'anic sense, given that the Arabs set themselves up as lords and masters, made male inhabitants into prisoners and women into objects of pleasure, while exploiting the region's resources. Was not all of this a military operation brought about by the expansion of the empire and deriving its legitimacy from Islam? In other words, did the propagation of a religion require the use of violence to guide people in the way of righteousness? A glance at the map of the Islamic world is sufficient to dispel any doubts: nearly three-fifths of Muslims live in regions which embraced Islam in a peaceful manner, through trade, the presence of the 'ulamā' and members of Sufi fraternities in regions such as Indonesia, China and large tracts of the Indian subcontinent and sub-Saharan Africa. This clearly shows that Islam does not rely on the use of force in order to spread and that worldly, material considerations were the real motives for the wars waged by the first generations of Muslims against neighbouring countries. There has always been a reluctance to describe these operations for what they were in reality – occupation, invasion, colonisation (to use modern terminology) – considering them instead as a combat waged in God's name, in accordance with His will and the *sunna* (practice) of His Prophet. As a result, the defensive forays carried out by the Prophet to safeguard the very existence of the nascent religion were interpreted as being offensive in intent, and were assimilated to the campaigns subsequently waged by Muslims. These latter campaigns thus acquired a legitimacy that they would not otherwise have possessed. The point of view of Sufyān al Thawri,[22] who held that fighting with the polytheists was obligatory only when they themselves initiated hostilities remained an exception among 'ulamā' and political figures.

Recognition of historical reality does not mean denying the good faith of those who carried out the conquests. They were confident that they were in the right, and that they were merely carrying out the instructions of the Prophet. One can also readily recognise that many of those who took part in the conquest sacrificed their lives and resources in a noble cause, and in God's name, hoping merely for reward in the world to come. This does not mean that other aspects of the situation or the latent reasons behind the conquests should be ignored. They constituted a clear deviation from the aims of the message of Islam: *jihād*, in its violent, aggressive form (together with the iniquities which resulted) prevailed at the expense of freedom of conscience and the call to a better life.[23] It may well be that the spread of Islam could have taken on a more positive form, without violence and exploitation. Perhaps it would have been more firmly implanted in the hearts of believers, and would have had less need of states and governments and institutions which call people to account and practice intellectual and even physical forms of terrorism. It is not a question of going back over the past and hauling previous generations before the tribunal of history on account of their actions; one can, however, demystify human history and, free from any lingering complexes, examine its merits and failures without exaggerating them.

2

Institutionalised Islam

The core beliefs and initial message of all religions tend to undergo a process of organisation and institutionalisation, and Islam was no exception in this respect. The basic principles of the message of Islam could not take form in the setting of the history of the first/seventh century without undergoing a similar process. Institutionalisation involves passing from theory to application, from what is potentially present to that which exists in reality. This inevitably means that first principles will lose a greater or lesser degree of their initial élan, and acquire characteristics that reflect a specific historical situation with all its ramifications and contradictions. One should not be surprised to find that one of many potential or existing interpretations attracts the adhesion of individuals or groups, prevails over the others and marginalises them, gradually acquiring the status of authentic and self-evident truth. This is because the interpretation in question conforms to ways of thinking at that time and to the prevailing balance of socio-economic and political power.

There were three main orientations in this process: first, differentiation from other groups, stressing what separated Muslims from other communities, be they polytheists or *ahl al-kitāb*. This is unsurprising, given that the Muslims were initially a minority among the inhabitants of the conquered territories, afraid of being absorbed into the religious and racial mix surrounding them. They, therefore, needed to create ways in which they would easily recognise one another in matters of dress, clothes and general conduct. One manifestation of this desire for distinction was the obligation placed on the *dhimmis* (Jewish and Christian minorities) to wear distinctive dress. They were also forbidden to ride on horseback, and restrictions were placed on the construction of churches and synagogues, along with other measures known as "the clauses of 'Umar".[1] Their attribution to 'Umar and the extent of their application are questionable. The need for the *fuqahā'* to underline the need for these measures may be proof of their non-application. The proclamation of such measures could also be a means, together with the abolition of taxes, for rulers to curry favour with the common people when necessary. In general the *status quo ante* was soon restored.[2]

Muslims behaved more or less similarly to the followers of other religions when, after the death of the individual bearing their initial message, and, thanks to those who were the effective founders of these religions, they formed communities possessing shared rites, beliefs and taboos. One could cite as examples Ezra, after the Babylonian exile in the sixth century BCE, in the case of Judaism, and Paul and his non-Jewish disciples in the case of Christianity. This tendency to form a separate community manifested itself progressively among the Muslims from the period of 'Umar onwards as a direct result of the expansion of the territories under their control and the spread of Muslim populations across these regions. One should, however, note that the formation of a Muslim community with a pattern of behaviour distinct from that of other religious communities was a phenomenon affecting city dwellers rather than country people. Rural dwellers became Muslims and discovered Islam's texts, rites and code of conduct at a later period.[3] Rural societies were more cohesive, and strategies of differentiation more difficult to implement. When Islam spread into rural areas it was inconceivable to imagine women being obliged to wear the veil or being confined to their homes as happened in urban settings. This shows that the desire for difference comes up against limits, connected with social conventions and established ways of life. It takes on a religious coloration in function of the surrounding environment, and its legislation aims to exclude the "other" focusing on what divides people rather than what unites them in complementary, supportive groups.

Institutionalisation also meant transforming varying forms of worship into uniform liturgies in which there was no scope for personal initiative or departure from a number of unchanging principles. Ritualism is a phenomenon present in all religions. Islam in its historical form did not constitute an exception and gradually the idea took hold among Muslims that worship, in the forms of prayer, fasting, and pilgrimage could be carried out only in a set manner. Certain elements were obligatory, others traditional, while yet others were supererogatory, to be carried out voluntarily. If, as we have previously noted, the message of Islam was initially marked by considerable flexibility in this respect, this tended to disappear, with the way that the Prophet prayed held to be binding in all its details. In reality these details were not stable during the life of the Prophet, and varied due to a number of external factors. This explains, to some extent, the divergences which subsequently arose, pitting the imāms and their followers from one legal school against those belonging to another school. Certain details were given preference over others, and the collective Muslim memory retained only those about which there was a consensus or an approximate version thereof, leaving aside the question of whether the Prophet had in fact observed these details or was merely imagined by the community to have done so. The Muslims, and their 'ulamā' in particular, did not have a natural propensity toward a uniform ritual, but they could envisage no other way of safeguarding the unity of the community. The sects which developed under the caliphate of 'Ali also sought to give their ritual distinctive characteristics, some of which caused violent strife. The Shī'a, for example, insist on employing the formula "Come and accomplish the worthiest action", while the Sunnis refuse this.[4] It occurred to no one to leave Muslims free to worship in the way that seemed the most appropriate, as society at that time did not look on pluralism and variety as sources of enrichment, without which human existence soon loses its flavour. Diversity was a source of apprehension, and treated with the utmost wariness. The result was that formalism triumphed over fervour and devotion, sincerity and spontaneity. Prayer became a series of bows and prostrations at set times of the day, mechanical actions carried out by the person praying, often in ignorance of their significance and intent. In the majority of Muslim societies, the Ramadhan fast has come to mean abstaining from food and drink and reducing physical effort during the day, while overeating in the evening to the point of being unwell. Late nights and cheap entertainment complete this unprepossessing tableau. As for the pilgrimage, it is merely a set of unchanging rites which take no account of the number of people involved, or distinguish between long, dangerous and fatiguing journeys or swift and undemanding ones.

The growth of this ritualism was one of the most important reasons behind the growth of Sufism on the margins of institutionalised Islam, because of dissatisfaction with the merely external forms of piety imposed by the *fuqahā'*. Sufism subsequently evolved into a constellation of fraternities around which developed all manner of affiliations while fulfilling a number of symbolic and practical functions, especially when central authority weakened and the fabric of society began to unravel both in the Maghreb and the Mashreq. The Sufis reacted critically to the exorbitant wealth of the upper class as well as to the empty superficiality of a prosperous society such as that of the Abbasids. At the same time, the dutiful performance of rituals did not provide the Sufis with sufficient spiritual sustenance. A number of leading Sufis rejected ritualism, although a majority adopted a more conciliatory attitude. From the beginning of the third/ninth century the Sufis belonging to the Sunni school prevailed over their opponents, and managed to balance the competing demands of "Law" and "Truth", and reconcile the respect of external reality with the desire to explore the inner depths of the soul. However, they remained tolerant of popular piety with its multiple expressions in which the imagination played an important role. These included the intercession and mediation of holy men and women, bodily expression, the performance of set collective rites, recitation of the Qur'an, litanies, and the invocations associated with each *tarīqa* or Sufi spiritual "family".[5]

The third consequence of the institutionalisation of religion was the formation of a series of binding dogmas. It is evident that it is not possible to make a comparison with Christianity in this respect as Islam has no need of dogmas concerning subjects such as the Trinity, the incarnation, salvation, original sin and other matters which give rise to disparate and conflicting interpretations. Dogmas nevertheless developed within Islam which, with the passage of time, became set in stone. These often concerned the rules associated with what was considered to be correct conduct rather than the content of faith itself. Shī'ites became convinced of the centrality of the imamate restricted to Ali and his descendants, while the Sunnis replied by stressing the primacy of the "rightly-guided" caliphs, according to the chronological order of their succession to the leadership of the Muslim community. Both groups considered that the Qur'an contained a series of prescriptions to be applied in a literal manner, regardless of the time and place. This gradually led to the formation of a unchanging system of thought and practice which was considered the *Sunna* of the Prophet, similar to the Qur'an insofar as it was held to be divinely inspired, although in a different manner. This in turn led to a strict delimitation of the methods of interpreting the text, relying heavily on analogy (*qiyās*).

The traditions recounting the words of the Prophet were assigned a position of unassailable authority, being considered the "way leading to knowledge" (*jihat-al-'ilm*). The authority of the first two generations who transmitted the traditions (the *Sahāba* or Companions, and the *Tābi'ūn* or Followers) was unchallengeable, although that of subsequent generations could be contested. A rapid survey of the dogmas of the *Sunna* reveals how Muslims were compelled to accept a collection of "eternal truths" which had originally been the object of controversy. A whole range of subjects including the creation of the Qur'an, belief in the preordaining of human acts towards good or evil and the concomitant denial of human freedom to choose, an irrational view of social and natural phenomena, the arbitrary nature of divine approval, the perception of God in this world or the next, the punishment of the tomb, the questioning of the believer by Munkar and Nākir,[6] the infallibility of the Companions, to name but a few, were considered to be self-evident truths. This delimitation of what Muslims must believe serves only to validate the solutions adopted by the dominant intellectual class of the time, and to close off avenues of debate and dissension so as to perpetuate the power of the 'ulamā' and the representatives of the religious establishment. There was no room for free thought or informed individual search for answers to existential and metaphysical questions; questions to which no one can claim to possess precise and complete answers.

This third aspect of the institutionalisation of religion did not manifest itself clearly from the beginning, since the transformation of a religion into an institution always takes place gradually. There is an initial stage of spontaneous piety whose form is not imposed from the outside. Institutionalisation requires the formation of a group exclusively or primarily occupied with religious matters. Such a development became necessary in a society transformed by the conquests where there was a natural tendency toward specialisation as Islamic civilisation became more prosperous and complex. There was also a need for a pact between this religious group and the holders of political power who monopolised the legal use of violence. Whatever may have been the degree of independence enjoyed by these "men of religion" in relation to the holders of political power – and many shied away from authority, declining even the post of *qādi* and other official titles – the divergence was not between the interests of the political and religious notables but rather between this politico-religious establishment and the mass of the people, including women and slaves, who were deprived of any kind of authority, even if they formed the majority of the population. Religious notables could be of non-Arab origin (*mawāli*) or of lowly origin, but once they obtained official recognition, they belonged henceforth to the elite and enjoyed its privileges. Political and religious elites needed each other's support, which gave rise to negotiation, compromise, and sometimes conflict, especially with the founding of the Abbasid empire (749–1258/132–656) which used religious ideology to buttress its legitimacy.

The study of these three areas – distinction between Muslims and non-Muslims, the formalising of ritual and the development of dogma – leads the observer to the conclusion that the diversion of the message of Islam caused by the process of institutionalisation is part of a common trend affecting any message or programme, religious or otherwise. Any attempt to realise these in history has quite unexpected results, different from what was foreseen. People's opinions and behaviour cannot be programmed in advance like a machine, or foreseen as animal behaviour can be, governed as it is by instinct. Changing external circumstances affect the way people act, and they are influenced by their needs, be they psychological or cultural, which have varied from one milieu to another. It is possible that the increase in the number of Muslims may have been a cause of qualitative decline, insofar as institutional or organised religion tolerates the natural tendency of ordinary believers to content themselves with the bare minimum of observance, which consists of performing external rituals while adopting an unforgiving attitude toward tendencies which seem to threaten its structures. This religious "establishment" refuses any individual appropriation of religion, or a return to the ideals of the founding generation.

In other words, it is a mistake to unquestioningly follow in every detail the path mapped out by the early generations of Muslims who sought to put the message of the Prophet into practice. Their understanding of the message was conditioned by their context and they interpreted it according to their interests, their intellectual horizons and the conflicts in which they found themselves caught up. Imitation of previous generations and fear of innovation were not so much a phenomenon accompanying early applications of Islamic teaching as the product of other factors, including the balance of forces which resulted from the victory of the *hadīth* party over their Mu'tazalite adversaries at the beginning of the caliphate of al-Mutawakkil (232–247/845–861).[7]

One should evaluate critically the positions defended by the first generations of Muslims, especially when one recalls the contradictory opinions attributed to distinguished members of these generations. This was not due to an evolution in their thought, or a change brought about by external events, but because of the way in which, from the beginning of the second/eighth century onwards illustrious names surrounded by a halo of sanctity were brandished in order to give credibility to the *hulūl*[8] defended by the *fuqahā'* and the *hadīth* scholars. Two

examples illustrate this. The *hadīth* collections give a privileged place to the traditions transmitted by Abū Huraira despite his having accompanied the Prophet
for only a few months. His conduct at the time of Mu'awiya was not a model of
rectitude.[9] The books of exegesis (*tafsīr*), such as those of Tabari and those who
followed in his footsteps, are full of traditions attributed to 'Abdallah ibn Abbās,
who, although he was a scholar, was also a participant in the conquests, being
one of the seven 'Abdallahs involved in the first expedition against Ifrīqiya. He
was active in politics, although his conduct when he was appointed governor of
Kufa by Ali was far from noble. In addition, his age – he was around twelve when
the Prophet died– made him too young to have been a Companion in the precise
sense of the word or a trustworthy witness to the events that took place at the
time of the revelation. It would have been inconceivable in the Abbāsid period
to accuse the "ancestor of the caliphs" of lying or to question the pertinence of
his opinions, supposing for a moment that they were true or partially true.[10]

The institutionalised version of Islam which is the subject of this chapter,
and which has survived until the present day, is that which progressively took
form once the situation stabilised in the second/eighth century, after the trans-
formations which took place during the life of the Prophet and the following
decades. The first generation of Muslims had, due to the Conquests, lived
through swift and far-reaching changes in all areas of their lives. They emerged
from relative isolation in the Arabian peninsula and found themselves mingling
with peoples who had their own beliefs, moral codes, customs, traditions and
social organisation.

Naturally the Arabs were influenced by all of this, and Islamic trappings
were given to many of these cultural elements (as long as they did not counter
the basic principles of the new religion) in areas which the Qur'an had passed
over in silence or for which there was no precedent in revelation. By living in
the conquered lands, and intermarrying with their inhabitants, they discovered
other civilisations, of which some were superior to their own, together with ways
of life, systems of thought and sensibilities far removed from those to which they
were accustomed.[11] Knowledge, crafts and techniques spread among the Arabs
as they adopted urban lifestyles and passed from a lifestyle of simple necessities
to one of convenience (*al-hājji*) and luxury (*al-kamāli*) to use the terms of Ibn
Khaldoun (732–808/1332–1406).[12] Their leaders and notables also went from a
life of austerity to one of luxury and abundant wealth. They founded an imperial
state and were subjected to a central government in Medina, then in Damascus,

and finally Baghdad which could either act as a substitute for the moral authority of the tribal chief, or leave him certain prerogatives.

It was to be expected that these and other changes would have an effect on the Islamic system that was taking form. Muslims, however, generally refused to acknowledge this, despite the profound and obvious effect of these trans-formations. This explains why, at the time of the Abbasid Caliphate, attempts were made to construct an historical theory which glossed over the historical factors driving these changes. Scholars sought to affirm continuity between the period of the Prophet and the period when the new institutions had developed. The result was that their image of the message of Islam was not one that took account of the message, its logic and its intentions. Their Islam was the distilla-tion of more than a century's practice and application, a reading of the Qur'an and an interpretation of the Prophet's life according to the views and the value system of their period, within the interpretative framework that had taken form over more than a century using standard models of thought, common to the cultures of the region.[13] Herein resides the difficulty of our undertaking, aiming as it does to explore this obscure period and strip away the accumulation of commonplace clichés to reveal the reality. It is an attempt to delve into what has been eliminated, deliberately forgotten, confused, or deformed, striving also to discover why certain solutions enjoy legitimacy while others do not, while yet others went unnoticed by Muslims and their scholars. One may also wonder why certain solutions were the object of reflection for outstanding scholars, but did not find a favourable environment in which account might have been taken of them.

Observe, for example, the following brief extract from the *I'lām* of al-'Amīrī, where he discusses the art of *fiqh*:

> Although personal interpretations may have been forbidden, for imāms there are only two alternatives: affirming, as do the "Twelvers" or *Imāmīs*, that the imām is infallible or recognising that what is approved by reason is licit, as al-Nazzām stated. The infallible imām will not be replaced and should the need arise there will be no possibility of having recourse to him. As for adopting what reason suggests, this is, in the eyes of the Hanbalites and Imamites, a major heresy. The only solution is, therefore, to go back to the source, retaining the practices of the best of the Companions.[14]

Al-ʿĀmirī does not explain how one can dispense with the infallible imām and the "practices of the best of the Companions" and rely on reason alone. He does not consider "declaring licit what reason approves" to be heresy in itself, although it was seen as such by the Hanbalites and the Imamites. In the end he does not retain this rational principle as he sought elements of unity and not division. This brief allusion suffices to show that certain Muslims in the third/ ninth century believed that humans did not need a divine law, whatever its source, in order to help society to function. In other words, there was no contradiction between Islam and existing laws: in this respect they can be described as pioneering "secular" thinkers. For this reason their opinions were marginalised and forgotten, or deliberately overlooked, and their contemporaries took no notice of the potentialities of their thought or the horizons that it could have opened up. For this to happen agreement would have been needed on rational efforts to organise society and the message of Islam would not have been transformed into legal corpus.

A detailed study of the period following the death of the Prophet up until the middle of the second/eighth century, a period for which there exist only secondary sources, is beyond the scope of this book. Nor is it possible to study all the ways in which Muslim practice diverged from the objectives of the message. This would require monographs on the different areas of Islamic thought as it took form before its codification in treatises and collections which have acquired the status of authoritative reference works. These include the *Sīra* of Ibn Isḥāq and Ibn Hishām, the *Tabaqāt* of Ibn Saʿd, *al-Fiqh al-akbar* of ʾAbu Ḥanīfa, the *Muwaṭṭaʾ* of Mālik, the *Risāla* of Shāfiʿi, the *Ṣaḥīḥ* of Muslim and the *Tafsīr* of Tabari.[15] These Muʿtazilite, Sunnite and Shīʿite volumes on *fiqh, tafsīr, hadīth*, the science of *kalām*, along with the Sufi literature, are the sole existing sources for the study of Islamic thought.

On the basis of these sources we shall concentrate our efforts on the major orientations and turning points of Islamic thought. We shall bring together a number of specific examples, representing the major themes treated by Islamic literature, even if it is difficult to present an abridged version of these themes without distorting them, given their varied and abundant nature. It is vain to use texts and quotations as weapons of controversy; what really matters is to try to better understand historical events without unwittingly adopting positions based on preconceptions and apologetic glorification, which serve neither truth nor learning.

3
The Elaboration of Institutional Theory

H aving studied how Islam inevitably took on the characteristics of an
institutional religion, we can go on to demonstrate how this affected
the theories elaborated by Muslim scholars in the different fields of
Islamic thought. These fields were not, originally, independent of one another;
tafsīr, for example, was not an autonomous speciality, nor were *hadīth* or *fiqh*
clearly defined. The areas of theological research were not yet delimitated, while
the study of the origins of *fiqh* came into being only after the development of *fiqh*
itself in order to set out the methods by which laws could be established through a
process of deduction. These questions were interconnected and complementary,
and were responses to practical questions arising in specific circumstances. They
were not the outcome of specialised study or abstract calculation. The multiplicity of problems confronting the first generations of Muslims led them to find
timely solutions which were intended to give a distinctive identity to the Muslim
community and foster internal solidarity. Factors of division were numerous:
racial origin; social standing; language or dialect; as well as contrasting cultures,
economic and administrative institutions, and other diverging interests. In these
circumstances, it was natural to reduce the manifestations of disunity and strive,
insofar as possible, for a unified code of conduct and shared inner convictions.
The message announced by the Prophet dealt with only a very small number
of questions, while the texts, however varied their interpretation, were limited
in contrast to the boundless variety of human history. The construction of an
organised, coherent structure with a religious foundation was an urgent task.
After hesitation, stumbling and controversy the Muslim community set about

this task. With the passage of time a structure of thought and practice began to take form.

Nevertheless, it is an illusion to believe that the *fiqh* developed by the 'ulamā' at the time of codification and the earlier solutions adopted by the first generation of believers are complementary. This belief is based on the impression of continuity created by the uninterrupted chains (*isnād*) of transmitters of *hadīth* and the exploitation of the traditions as arguments to support particular points of view, as though these traditions were free from any trace of falsification, deformation, inaccurate recall, carelessness, or negligence. The founders of Islam, and particularly the first generation of believers at the time of the "simple faith", to use the expression of Ibn Khaldoun, were primarily interested in practical solutions, which varied according to the circumstances and the people and issues involved. It would not have occurred to them that these solutions needed to be uniform or that they needed a religious guarantee in order to be acceptable and applicable.[1]

To underline this point of view we put forward as an example the standpoint expounded by Ibn Khaldoun when he criticises the errors of the historians. The reader will excuse this lengthy quotation from the beginning of the *Muqaddimah* as it is a perfect expression of the methodology appropriate to the subject under discussion. Ibn Khaldoun writes thus on the:

> excellence of historiography, an appreciation of the various approaches to history, a glimpse of the different kinds of errors to which historians are liable, and some of the causes which result in errors, notes that 'the writing of history needs numerous sources and greatly varied knowledge. It requires a good speculative mind and thoroughness. Possession of these two qualities leads the historian to the truth and keeps him from slips and errors. If he trusts historical information in its plain, transmitted form and has no clear idea of the principles resulting from custom, the fundamental facts of politics, nature of civilisation or the conditions governing human social organisation, and if, furthermore, he does not evaluate remote or ancient material through comparison with near or contemporary material, he often cannot avoid stumbling and slipping and deviating from the highroad of truth. Historians, Qur'an commentators and leading transmitters have committed frequent errors in the stories and events they reported. They accepted them in the plain transmitted form, without regard for its value. They did not check them with the principles

underlying such historical situations, nor did they compare them with similar material. Also, they did not probe more deeply with the yardstick of philosophy, with the help of knowledge of the nature of things, or with the help of speculation and historical insight. They strayed from the truth and found themselves lost in the desert of baseless assumptions and errors.[2]

Having given examples of what he considered error and illusion, Ibn Khaldoun adds:

> The scholar needs to know the principles of politics, the true nature of existent things and the differences among nations, places and periods with regard to ways of life, character, qualities, customs, sects, schools, and everything else. He needs a comprehensive knowledge of present conditions in all these respects. He must compare similarities in certain cases and differences in others. He must be aware of the differing origins and beginnings of different dynasties and religions, as well as of the reasons and incentives that brought them into being and the circumstances and history of the people that supported them. His goal must be to have complete knowledge of the reasons for every happening, and be acquainted with the origin of every event. Then he must check transmitted information with the basic principles he knows. If it fulfils their requirements, it is sound. Otherwise the historian must consider it as spurious and dispense with it … a hidden pitfall in historiography is disregard for the fact that conditions within the nations and races change with the change of periods and the passing of days. This is a sore affliction and deeply hidden, becoming noticeable only after a long time; rarely do more than a few individuals become aware of it. The condition of the world and of nations, their customs and sects, does not persist in the same form or in a constant manner. There are differences according to days and periods, and changes from one condition to another. This is the case with individuals, times and cities and in the same manner it happens in connection with regions and districts, periods and dynasties.[3]

In the first book of the *Muqadimmah* concerned with the nature of civilisation, Ibn Khaldoun starts by outlining the ways in which untruth affects historical information:

Untruth naturally affects historical information. There are various reasons
which make this unavoidable. One of them is partisanship for opinions
and schools. If the soul is impartial in receiving information, it devotes
to that information the share of critical investigation the information
deserves, and its truth or untruth thus becomes clear. However if the soul
is infected with partisanship for a particular opinion, it accepts without
a moment's hesitation the information that is agreeable to it. Prejudice
and partisanship obscure the critical faculty and preclude critical investigation, with the result that falsehoods are accepted and transmitted. Another
reason making untruth unavoidable in historical information is reliance
on transmitters ... while another is unawareness of the purpose of events,
unfounded assumptions as to the truth of a thing. This is frequent and
caused by reliance on transmitters. Another reason is ignorance of how
conditions conform to reality. They are often affected by ambiguities and
artificial distortions. The fact is that people as a rule approach great and
high-ranking persons with praise and encomia. They embellish conditions
and spread the fame of great men. The information made public in such cases
is not truthful. Another reason making untruth unavoidable, and one that
is more powerful than all the reasons previously mentioned, is ignorance of
the various conditions arising in civilisation. Every event (or phenomenon)
whether it comes into being in connection with some essence as the result
of an action, must inevitably possess a nature peculiar to its essence as to
the accidental conditions that may attach themselves to it. If the student
knows the nature of events and the circumstances and requirements in the
world of existence, it will help him to distinguish truth from untruth in
investigating the historical information critically ... it is superior to inves-
tigations that rely upon criticism of the personalities of transmitters. Such
personality criticism should not be resorted to until it has been ascertained
whether a particular piece of information is in itself possible or not. If it is
absurd there is no use engaging in personality criticism.[4]

One might think that this text was written yesterday rather than over six
centuries ago, as it shows little sign of its antiquity, and were it not for certain
stylistic features one might attribute it to a contemporary author should one
ignore its source. Ibn Khaldoun was, however, labouring under a handicap (one
that was psychological in nature, although also a consequence of the prevailing

mentality of his time) which prevented him from applying his method to traditions linked to the religious sciences. This leads him to affirm, after his preceding description of the direct causes of falsehood, that:

> personality criticism is only taken into consideration in connection with the soundness or lack of soundness of Muslim religious information, because this religious information contains injunctions in accordance with which the lawgiver (Muhammad) enjoined Muslims to act whenever it can be presumed that the information is genuine. The way to achieve presumptive soundness is to ascertain the probity and exactness of the transmitters.[5]

He sums up his position at the end of the chapter which he devotes to *hadīth* sciences: "Of all people scholars most deserve that one may have a good opinion of them and that one be eager to find sound excuses for them."[6]

If this is the case, the time has come to overcome the handicap which led Ibn Khaldoun to distort reality when he claims that the prescriptions of Muslim law are, for the most part, arbitrary prescriptions. Consultation of any volume of *fiqh*, *tafsīr*, (Qur'anic exegesis) or *hadīth* from the second or third centuries after the Hijra will reveal the inaccuracy of this affirmation. These prescriptions are contained within traditions guaranteed by a chain (*isnād*) of transmitters going back in some cases to the Prophet and most of the time to the Companions, the Followers and particularly the imāms of the schools of jurisprudence. Arbitrary prescriptions cannot be separated from tradition.[7] Ibn Khaldoun makes the very error that he himself denounces in the non-religious domain, namely "partisanship for a particular opinion" or "reliance on transmitters" or "ignorance of the nature of various conditions in civilization", in the Khaldounian sense of this latter term, which includes social institutions, crafts, science and learning. It is less a question of reliance on transmitters or considering them unreliable than an awareness of the errors to which any transmitter is prone: illusions, forgetfulness, error, or confusion can affect even a transmitter of tradition who strives to pass on what he has heard in an authentic and faithful manner without adding or omitting elements. No historian worthy of the name will today rely on the *isnād* or set any store by its presentation of past or present events, regardless of the sincerity, piety, competence and virtue with which the transmitters of the tradition are invested.[8]

No historian claims to possess absolute truth. Events and facts do not have a unique and objective way of existing, but take on meaning through the way in which they are perceived by each person according to their point of view, their faculties of perception and the context in which they exist. The historian produces the past as much as he or she narrates it. An historian, conscious of the limits of the knowledge available, will not only consider it with caution but will also be vigilant in examining the numerous material or intellectual factors which may influence the way in which events are interpreted. Without succumbing to sterile relativism, a correct and scholarly approach requires that the historian uncover the coherence of the elements available without projecting on to them contemporary or personal considerations, or making anachronistic judgments or appreciations. Certain elements of received wisdom of events in the first century of the Hegira need to be reexamined, especially when it comes to the question of how loyal the first generations of Muslims were to the principles of the message of Muhammad, as it was their vocation to embody these values.

We shall not repeat here what has already been noted about the conduct of the Prophet when faced with the responsibility of presiding over the destiny of the Muslim community during its incipient phase in Mecca and subsequent formative period in Medina. It is sufficient to mention the flexibility characterising his conduct, and his overall aim of educating Muslims in new ethical values going against many aspects of pre-Islamic customs, while on other occasions conforming to them, taking account of prevailing realities, proceeding gradually and giving priority to what was essential in the light of prevailing circumstances and the balance of forces.[9]

Arbitration between rival parties was one of the most important tasks of the Prophet, one that he exercised in person when circumstances required or that he delegated to certain of his Companions in remote regions, such as Yemen. After the death of the Prophet, the caliphs themselves assumed this duty in the empire's main centre and conferred this responsibility to *qādis* in the conquered territories. Inevitably, the traditional tribal instance of arbitration was superseded by the position of the *qādi*, who acted according to the requirements of the new central authority. The *qādi's* authority was no longer derived from the acceptance of his authority by the two parties, but was an extension of the political authority which had appointed him to that post. This same central authority would help him implement his judgments, by force if necessary.

These judges did not initially undergo any particular preparation, nor did they refer to a legal code similar to that promulgated by the Byzantine emperor, Justinian, in the sixth century CE. They were, for the most part, familiar to varying degrees with the precedents established by the Prophet or set out by revelation. However, not all these judges had been alive at the time of the various stages of revelation of the Qur'an nor had they witnessed personally the events of that period. The cases with which these *qādis* had to deal were more numerous than existing precedents and certain of them were more complicated, related to socio-economic problems very different from those of the Prophet's time and involving people whose ethical values, customs, traditions and ways of life were very different from those of the Arabs in the Hejaz and in the Arabian peninsula as a whole. The inhabitants of Iraq, Persia, Syria and Egypt had inherited civilisations and institutions of a high degree of refinement, while life in the fertile agricultural basins of the great rivers (Nile, Tigris, and Euphrates) was thus very different from that in arid desert regions. This context shaped social relations and the way in which people envisaged the functions of central government and its representatives, such as tax collectors, judges and other agents of central authority.

Muslim *qādis*, therefore, sought to adapt to these circumstances, recognising numerous practices of the peoples of the conquered territories when they did not seem to fundamentally contradict the principles of the new religion. On the other hand, they attempted to apply the customs that they had known in their own Arab environment. Some *qādis*, for practical reasons, sought to familiarise themselves with the legal provisions existing in the conquered regions particularly in relation to taxes and administration, and thus acquired expertise in Jewish, Byzantine and Persian law. This, among other elements, explains the degree of resemblance between the Muslim judicial system and laws existing around the Mediterranean basin region.[10] It was only natural, in the absence of any detailed texts and codified criteria, that the judgments made should vary from place to place, according to temperament, nature, persons and circumstances. This was a cause of unease among governors and subjects alike, especially as the questions dealt with concerned not only the usual insignificant disputes but involved blood feuds, crimes of honour and other vital interests and could lead to the validation or the invalidation of religious ritual.

Fiqh

These inconsistencies in the decisions made by *qādis* were destined to make an enduring mark on *fiqh*, although scholars initially endeavoured to bridge the gap between contradictory practices and coordinate the various decisions made in different regions of the Muslim world. Their attempts to produce a coherent system followed the same rationale as the expanding empire. This meant giving the Islamic community, destined to expand and absorb large numbers of communities and individuals, a more or less unified system of worship and practices governing social relations. The diversity of the empire's subjects and their origins prevented the complete harmonisation of legislation. 'Ulamā' in each metropolis, especially in the Hejaz, Syria and Iraq, strove to demonstrate the sound foundations for their decisions and furnish justifications for them. Traditions attributed to the Prophet and handed down by a chain of transmitters were used to support particular solutions and present them in a favourable light.

This observation may lead the historian to relativise the dispute between the champions of personal opinion and discernment (*ahl al-ray*), on the one hand, and *hadīth* scholars, on the other hand. This dispute developed in the second century of the Hegira, gathering strength in the third/ninth century as *imāms* came to prominence for each school of jurisprudence. Their disciples took it upon themselves to defend their masters' opinions. Personal opinion and free interpretation prevailed immediately after the time of the Prophet, and continued to do so unchallenged at least throughout the first/seventh century, in the absence of systematic recourse to the text of the Qur'an, or to the acts or declarations of the Prophet concerning great or small issues. The drawing of analogies between past and present, or between cases arising (*far'*)[11] and an existing precedent (*asl*), to use the terminology of the *fuqahā'*, was not an established practice. This explains why *fiqh*, even after taking on a fixed and codified form, remained a peculiarly dense mass of cases divided into sections and chapters. It is well-nigh impossible to ground these individual cases in all-embracing general principles which explain their different parts and details. The law codes are evidence of this. There is no trace in the vast *fiqh* literature of any attempt to explain reasons or aims. It did not prove possible to establish a legislative structure in the precise sense of this term. It may, however, have made possible a kind of balanced interaction between members of society, based on trust, a moral rather than a juridical quality, or on threats and coercion, which produce results contrary to mutual concord and tolerance.

One should not be misled by one juridical school's acceptance of a particular source of *fiqh*, particularly consensus or analogy, while another school refuses it. This happened in the case of the Hanafite and Zahirite schools, as well as the Ja'afarite and Hanbalite. The disagreement between these schools does not concern the solutions which each may accept, but has to do rather with the justification for these solutions. Whether one turns to the *Mudawwana* of the Malekite scholar, Sahnūn (d. 240/850), the *Muhallā* of the Zahirite, Ibn Hazm (d. 453/1063), or even the *Daʾāim* of the Ismailian qādi, al-Nuʿumān (d. 363/971), one finds differences over the basis for the legal prescriptions. In one case it may be a tradition originating with a Shīʿa *imām*, in another the tradition will be handed down by a single unbroken line of transmitters. Sahnūn relies on the opinion of Mālik and Ibn al-Qāsim and on existing practice in Medina. The divergences between these sources are no more considerable than those existing between the *Umm* of al-Shāfiʿī (d. 202/819), the *Mabsūt* of the Hanefite, al-Shaybani (d. 189/804) or the *Mughni* of the Hanbalite, Ibn Qudama (d. 620/1223). The *fiqh* elaborated by these schools retained a large proportion of the contradictory solutions which characterised the initial period of Islamic history, while giving them an Islamic veneer. It is clear that they were the product of particular circumstances, which in their turn created convergences and differences between the solutions adopted.

Arab readers may be generally aware that Mālik declined the offer of the caliph Mansūr to make the *Muwatta'* an official basis for Abbasid political and juridical decisions. They will also have heard of the famous debate between the Caliph Ma'mūn and a Zoroastrian, an event of which the Caliph was particularly proud. He supported implicitly the point of view of Mālik, that the differences between Muslims concern the branches and not the origin. This does not harm the soundness of religion or belief but rather opens up wider possibilities for interpretation. Numerous works deal with the question of divergences between the *fuqahāʾ*, the most widely-known being *Bidāyat al-mudjtahid wa nihāyat al-muqtasid* by Ibn Rushd in the sixth/twelfth century, and *rahmat al'umma fī ikhtilāf al-aʾimma* by the Shāfiʿite, al-Dimashqi in the eighth/fourteenth century.[12] Without going into details about subjects, such as the famous Hanefite capacity to find ways around the application of legal sanctions or the disputed legitimacy of *talfīq* (choosing between the decisions of the various schools), or the numerous inconclusive conferences and congresses organised to promote convergence between the schools, one may note that publications still appear today on the subject of divergences between schools, such as al-Jazīrī's *al-fiqh 'ala madhāhib al-arba'a* (Islamic jurisprudence according to the four schools). According to the dominant point of view *fiqh*, in all circumstances, and whatever the degree of discord between the *fuqahā'*, contains the "judgment of God", or the "judgment of canonical law".[13] Contrary as it may seem to all available evidence, one encounters the following affirmations: judgments made by the imāms of the various schools and their pupils are not human legislation as God alone is legislator. He is the source of all righteousness. Disagreement is, therefore, of little importance. These two articles of faith merit closer examination.

In order to go beyond mere theory, we shall quote the exact text of a number of examples from the aforementioned book of al-Dimashqi, illustrating the subjects about which the *fuqahā'* were in unanimous agreement as well as areas of disagreement. We can demonstrate their degree of fidelity to the divine law, bearing in mind our previous remarks about the ultimate aim of the preaching of Muhammad.

According to Mālik and Shā'fi'ī the prayer of a man who has a woman beside him is licit. Abū Hanīfa affirms that prayer in these circumstances is invalid.

There was a divergence of opinion concerning the presence of a river or a road separating the *imām* from the persons praying. According to Mālik and Shā'fi'ī, the latter may follow the *imām*, an opinion contradicted by Abū Hanīfa. If the believer prays at home while being guided by the *imām* who is in the mosque, and an obstacle prevents the believer from seeing the lines of people praying, Mālik and Shā'fi'ī and Ahmad ibn Hanbal agree that the prayer is not valid. Abū Hanīfa maintains that it is.

There is general agreement that the funeral prayer requires a state of ritual purity and the covering of the private parts. Sha'abi and Tabari maintain that the prayer is valid without the state of ritual purity.

There is general agreement that it is licit to pray for someone who has committed suicide. But according to al-Awzā'ī one should not. Qatāda says that one should not pray for an illegitimate child, while al-Hasan says that prayers should not be said for a woman giving birth.

If someone begins a journey after having started to fast, he is not allowed to break the fast, according to the three schools. But according to Ahmed ibn Hanbal, he may do so.

The sacrifice (*'aqīqa*) offered seven days after birth is a recognised precept in the eyes of Mālik and Shā'fi'ī Abū Hanīfa says "It is merely authorised. I would not say that it is desirable." Ahmed ibn Hanbal maintains that there are two traditions: the more well-known states that it is desirable, the other that it is obligatory. Certain of his disciples have chosen the latter. Al-Hasan and Daoud say that it is obligatory. The *'aqīqa* consists of the sacrifice of two sheep for a boy and one for a girl. According to Mālik, the sacrifice consists of the offering of one beast for a boy or a girl.

Can the house of a bankrupt person be sold if he cannot do without it? Abū Hanīfa and Ahmad ibn Hanbal reply no. The former adds: no part of his property or his livestock can be sold. On the contrary, say Mālik and Shā'fi'ī, all of these can be sold.

The *fuqahā'* belonging to the generation of the Companions and Followers in the various regions of the newly-conquered territories together with the imāms of the different schools agreed that the contracts of *musāqāt* are licit, although Abū Hanīfa declares that they are null and void.[14]

Another area of contention was that of relatives on the maternal side of a family to whom the Qur'an had not given the right to inherit. Mālik and Shāfi'ī deny them this right, adding that the inheritance should go to the Public Treasury. Abū Bakr, 'Umar, 'Uthmān, Zayd, al-Zuhri, al-Awzā'ī and Daoud share this point of view. On the contrary Abū Hanīfa and Ahmad recognise their right to inherit, according to a tradition recounted by 'Ali, Ibn Masoud and Ibn 'Abbās. There is unanimous agreement that this right can be exercised only in the absence of the inheritors mentioned by the Qur'an (*ashāb al-furūd*) and male inheritors.

According to Shāfi'ī and Ahmad, marriage is valid only when there is a male guardian. If a woman contracts a marriage by herself, it is invalid. Abū Hanīfa says that a woman has the right to contract a marriage or delegate this right if she is accustomed to looking after her own affairs. This can be opposed only when she envisages marriage with someone of inferior social condition. In that case the guardian can oppose the marriage. Mālik maintains that if the woman belongs to that class of woman sought in marriage because of their nobility and their beauty, a guardian is necessary. Should this not be the case, she may consent to a person outside her family assuming the role of guardian.

According to Shāfi'ī, Ahmad, and Abū Hanīfa, marriage is valid only when witnesses are present. Mālik says that it is valid in their absence, although it must have a public character. The spouses must not give their consent in secret. Shāfi'ī,

Ahmad and Abū Hanīfa do not consider that secret consent invalidates the marriage as long as there are two witnesses.

Repudiation: is it a right reserved to men or not? Yes, say Shāfiʿī, Mālik and Ahmad ibn Hanbal, while Abū Hanīfa says that women too have this right.

All agree that the minimum duration of the period of pregnancy is six months, while disagreeing about its maximum period. Abū Hanīfa says two years, while Mālik mentions four, five, or even seven years. Shāʿfiʿ gives a figure of four years. Ahmad ibn Hanbal has two traditions on this subject, the more well-known gives the same period as Shāfiʿī, the other that of Abū Hanīfa.

Another area of disagreement concerns the case of a man who is seized by another man while a third person kills him. Abū Hanīfa and Shāfiʿ say that the punishment due is inflicted on the man who dealt the mortal blow, but not to the other, to whom a discretionary sanction is applied. Mālik says that they are both party to the crime of murder and should be punished accordingly if the assassin could only have killed his victim with the aid of his accomplice who seized the victim, and if this action rendered flight impossible. Ahmad ibn Hanbal, in two separate traditions, says that the murderer should be killed and his accomplice imprisoned for life, while in another tradition he says that both the assassin and his accomplice should be put to death.[15]

There is agreement that the blood-price (*diya*) for a free Muslim woman (as opposed to a slave) is half that of a free Muslim man. There is disagreement about whether or not in case of injury there is an equal blood-price.

In the case of involuntary homicide, all the schools agree that the tribe of the person who perpetrated the homicide has to pay the *diya* over a period not exceeding three years. They disagree about whether the guilty person is himself bound to make payments along with his tribe. They also disagree about whether or not the *diya* is a fixed sum, or determined according to the capacity for payment or left to the appreciation of the judge.

They also disagreed about the penalty for drinking wine: eighty-four lashes according to Abū Hanīfa and Mālik, while Shāfiʿī says forty. Ahmad ibn Hanbal quotes both these texts. They agree that the whip should be used to administer the punishment, although Shāʿfiʿī stipulates that the hands, sandals, or the fringe of a piece of clothing should be used.

Can a woman be a *qādi*? No, says Mālik, Shāfiʿī and Ahmad ibn Hanbal, although Abū Hanīfa replies that she can officiate in all cases in which the evidence of a woman is admissible, which in his view includes all cases except those involving legal sanctions and injury. According to Ibn Jarīr et-Tabari, it is possible for a woman to be a *qādi* in all circumstances.

From these examples one may draw the following conclusions:

(1) All of these questions lack a textual basis in the Qur'an, even if they were sometimes used by way of analogy and interpreted in particular ways. Contradictory *hadīth* are also quoted, with a chain of transmitters going back to the Prophet or one of his Companions. Such *hadīth* were very probably invented with the aim of giving credibility to solutions approved by the *imāms* of the legal schools.

(2) These questions concern worship as well relations within society. The first element addresses the legitimate concern of the Muslims to have unified liturgical practices, although the conferral of a quasi-sacred status on everyday social customs in a particular historical context was a development destined to subsequently hinder the evolution of Muslim societies when a changed context required a new basis for social interaction.

(3) The consequences of these disagreements could be grave, entailing as they sometimes did the validity or invalidity of religious obligations as in the case of a man praying in proximity to a woman, the fasting required of travellers, the validity or otherwise of sexual relations, as well as questions concerning the legal tutor and the witnesses to a marriage It could even be a question of life and death, as in the case of the assassin and his accomplice.

(4) It is clear that agreement or disagreement between the *fuqahā'* reflected prevailing values during the period when *fiqh* began to develop in Islamic societies sharing a certain number of distinctive traits and differing in other respects. The jurists were in agreement concerning the unequal blood-price for men and women, given their view of women in general. It may be that Abū Hanīfa and al-Tabari gave women the right to divorce and allowed them to be *qādis* because women in Iraq had a different position in society compared with that of women in the Hejaz or in Egypt.

(5) Tribal customs and certain rites existing in the Arabian peninsula also influenced the evolution of jurisprudence: examples could include collective tribal responsibility in the case of individual crime, or the practice of the *'aqīqa*. The general level of learning at the time also played a part in such matters as the upper limit placed on the period of pregnancy (to be sure that a child born after a divorce was not conceived out of wedlock) and the question of prayers for a woman in childbed.

(6) Last but not least these divergences show that the *fuqahā'*, in making judgments, took into account sometimes contradictory economic interests which led to disagreements about the inheritance due to relatives on the maternal side, the statutes concerning irrigation and the vexed question of the sale of the belongings of a person declared bankrupt, especially his house.

Leaving aside areas of agreement and disagreement between the *fuqahā'* it is possible to identify a number of common characteristics.

First, the *fuqahā'* wanted to preserve an appearance of conformity with rites and practices rather than develop an interior self-awareness which would guide Muslims toward good and make them hold evil in abhorrence. The needs of communal life prevailed over a sense of individual responsibility and duties rather than rights were given primacy. This was inevitable given their belief that Muslims were not all subject to the same degree of obedience to religious obligations. They took it upon themselves to speak in the name of God, possessing, as they thought, exclusive knowledge of God's will, of what pleases him, of what he holds in abhorrence and of what he forbids. What is more, they considered that "God did not want certain Muslims to understand His will and He did not impose it upon them" and that women, even in matters which most concerned them such as menstruation, were "subject to the will of God who wanted them to observe the rules concerning menstruation, on condition that the *mufti* pronounce a *fatwa* to this end."[16] This, in our opinion, is merely a result of a division of labour produced by a particular economic situation, and has no connection at all with the will of God.

Claims to exclusive knowledge by one group led inevitably to similar claims by others, and the followers of the various schools – Sunnis, Kharidjites, moderate or extremist Shī'ites – considered that their school was more knowledgeable about the truth than the others. The case of Sahnoun (160/777–240/855), leader of the Malekites in Aghlabid Ifrīqiya is a well-known illustration of this tendency: he hounded the Hanefites out of the study circles in the Kairouan mosque. This kind of conduct persisted until recently in Muslim countries whose inhabitants belonged to more than one legal school or to sects competing for legitimacy and followers. In this competition *fatwas* were used as a weapon by representatives of the various schools, to such an extent that a term was invented to describe this quarrel: the *tafāti* or "fatwa war". When the Sufis attained a dominant position, they looked down on the *fuqahā'* who themselves looked down on the mass of the people, especially women, children and slaves. They considered them as the "scholars of evil", comparable to a rock that falls into the source of a river: it does not drink the water and does not allow it to flow out towards the fields.[17] Philosophers in turn considered themselves better qualified than *tafsīr* scholars and theologians to understand and interpret religion.[18]

Secondly, the formation of a class of specialists who had the exclusive responsibility for "managing" sacred matters resulted in the deviation of this class away from their essential task toward the reprehensible behaviour denounced by al-Kindi, who described the religious scholars of his time as people who were:

> strangers to truth, although they deck themselves in its finery undeservedly. They want to control religion, and trade in it, although they are without faith, since he who trades in something sells it and he who sells something no longer has it in his possession. The trader in religion has no religion. The person who appropriated truth and called it infidelity deserves to be denied the solace of religion.[19]

Abū al Hasan al-'Amīrī confirmed the nature of this deviance, describing its manifestations:

> Since the *fuqahā'* have reduced the aims of their noble profession to the domination of the common people, the currying of favour with rulers, and the seizure of the property of the weak, and have given themselves the authority to abolish rights and dues, their profession has gone from being praiseworthy to being blameworthy.[20]

There are numerous testimonies to such deviance, unsurprising when one considers the difficulty involved in opposing those who claim to speak in God's name, and who form a class united in the defence of its interests, in the absence of an effective counterweight. This was the prevailing situation in ancient societies, be they Islamic or not.

Thirdly, the desire of the *fuqahā'* to imitate the founding fathers of the first generation led to the development of various traditions linked to behaviour completely unconnected to religion, but which became firmly established in Muslim codes of manners. The following anecdote, one of many, demonstrates the failings of this approach: "Iyādh recounts, having heard it from Malik, that the latter entered 'Abdallah ibn Sālih's house. 'Abdallah was governor of Medina.

He sat for a while, then invited those present to wash their hands and eat, saying: 'Begin with Abū 'Abdallah.' Malik replied: 'Abū Abdallah' – he meant himself – 'does not wash his hands.' 'Abdallah ibn Sālih asked: 'Why?' Malik answered: 'That is not what I learned from the scholars in our city. That is the custom of foreigners. When 'Umar ate, he wiped his hand on the soles of his feet.' He added: 'Do not order someone to wash his hand, because he would take that as being an obligation, and it is not the case. Abolish the foreign custom and revive that of the Arabs!'"[21]

This kind of approach, together with other factors, resulted in a way of thinking that gave little place to the analysis of natural causes, preferring to identify immediately a first cause, that is to say God, to whom illness and healing are attributed, while medicines and treatments have no effect. Those who have recourse to them are threatened with dire punishment, as in the following verses attributed to an Andalusian poet at the period of the Banu Nasr dynasty who ruled Grenada between 629/1231–897/1491:

He who thinks that he will cure disease with a remedy will receive a dire punishment;
    Cast aside all that you see, and entrust yourself to Him who is all-powerful, all-knowing.[22]

This is unsurprising, given the way that ignorance was built into a system, and that love of learning and a spirit of enquiry had been killed off since servile imitation had come to dominate intellectual life. In the words of a poet of the Hafsid era:

All science save that of the Qur'an is the work of miscreants, except hadīth and *fiqh*;
    Learning has its source in what has been handed down to us and all else is but devilish suggestion.[23]

Fourthly, the most serious consequence of the activities of the *fuqahā'* has been the progressive drift away from direct contact with the text of the Qur'an. Muslims give priority instead to secondary texts which claim to correctly deduce the teachings of the Qur'an, while in reality hindering personal understanding and independent reflection, free from external guidance and constraint. In the same way that the figure of the Prophet took on exaggerated proportions, and was invested with lofty and idealised characteristics, so too the leaders of the schools of jurisprudence became quasi-infallible in the eyes of many Muslims. No one dared to criticise them or draw attention to the way in which the historical context inevitably influenced their teachings.

One may also note two major lacunae in the work of the *fuqahā'*.[24] The first concerns the statutes about land ownership. Treatises of *fiqh* said little more than that the land belongs to those who cultivate it, with particular attention to questions of boundaries of land and water resources, pre-emption and endowment, as well as questions pertaining to land seized as booty (*fay'*) and conquered territories. It is not surprising that most cultivated land was collectively owned by the tribe unless it belonged to the state, in which case it was allotted to those whom the central authority wanted to reward. The exploitation of the land was entrusted to peasants in return for payment of a land tax or other form of tax. This situation had a number of consequences: private landholdings were rare, a stable agricultural class did not develop and neither the exploitation of land nor investment in its long-term viability were promoted. For these reasons, the introduction by the Ottomans in 1274/1858 of a land law represented a radical change in the way in which land was legally acquired. It removed the lacunae hitherto existing in this area of *fiqh* and was followed by laws organising land ownership in the various areas of the Islamic world, all derived to various degrees from the legislation existing in Western countries.[25]

Fiqh had lagged behind in land-related questions, and contributed to the deterioration of agriculture over the course of time in the Islamic world: unfair monopolies; inflation; disorder; malnutrition; famine; and epidemics. Hardly a year went by without chroniclers recording one or other of these disasters. Another consequence was that the prime beneficiaries of the new laws giving official property deeds to landowners were tribal chiefs in rural areas and notables and business leaders in towns, at the expense of ordinary tribespeople and peasants on land that was collectively "owned", although without any legally recognised title deeds.

The second lacuna in the work of the *fuqahā'* is in the political domain. During the first four centuries of Islamic history, little attention was given to the organisation of this essential aspect of social life. The *fuqahā'* did not seek to specify precise norms for organising state institutions, merely calling for obedience to be given to the holder of power, no matter how he had obtained or exercised this authority. Their fear of innovation and decision-taking unsanctioned by their forebears led them to neglect their function in the domain of governance. They also failed to keep up with changes in society which required new methods of legal procedure besides Qur'anic jurisprudence, such as the *mazālim* (tribunals), the *hisba* (supervision of markets and public morals) and, in modern times, the civil courts. Consequently, theologians took it upon themselves to make up for these insufficiencies with their study of the question of the imamate and the conditions governing it, although from a specialised point of view. A less fortunate consequence was that those in authority held unfettered sway over their subjects rarely following the requirements of justice and equity. When, in the fifth/eleventh century al-Māwardi founded a political jurisprudence, his *Statutes of Government* were an attempt to justify the past and confer legitimacy on present practices characterised for the most part by tyranny and the primacy of personal interests rather than laying down a rational system derived from Qur'anic principles. The *fuqahā'* had little awareness of the importance of the duty of which the Prophet in his wisdom had been a proponent: coming to the aid of the oppressed fellow believer or even the oppressor, bringing the latter to abandon tyranny. Nor did they consider, as Muhammad did, the ruler as a shepherd. Muhammad extended the sense of "shepherding" and gave the traditional term a novel interpretation: "each one of you is a shepherd". The *fuqahā'* went along with an imperial model of authority, glorifying the ruler and making him into a remote, unaccountable figure. In exchange for this unquestioning allegiance, they had a free hand in the organisation of society and through long established rites they embodied a guarantee of cohesion between groups and individuals.

The Origins of Jurisprudence

One might expect that the discipline known as *usūl al fiqh* would have dealt with theoretical dimensions which *fiqh* itself was unable to treat, dealing exclusively as it did with *furū'*. In reality the specialists in *usūl al fiqh* sought to clarify and set out the dynamics of deductive research, while defending the solutions of the first generations of Muslims and providing them with convincing justifications. Their aim was to limit and circumscribe the divergences existing between the decisions of the caliphs and *qādis* and subsequently the *fuqahā'*, for nearly two centuries. They certainly prevented this discord from diminishing the credibility of these decisions, although they were unable to develop another form of *fiqh*, or rather, another system of jurisprudence which would have sought to establish justice and order on different bases, despite the difficulty of the undertaking. It is true that the desire to give an Islamic gloss to solutions proposed by the *fuqahā'* to real difficulties or what were presented as such manifested itself before the time of the Imām Shāfiʿī at the end of the second century of the Hijra. Shāfiʿī was, however, instrumental in making this as yet inchoate aspiration into part of the Muslim "mind-set" and in regrouping its various disparate elements into a coherent whole.[26] From the time of the composition of Shāfiʿī's *Risāla* onwards, Muslims came to accept that there were four sources of jurisprudence: the Qur'an, *Sunna*, consensus and analogy. While a detailed study of each of these subjects goes beyond the bounds of the present study, it is possible to examine the extent to which they remained faithful to the message of Islam.

Relying on the text of the Qur'an in order to make deductions of a legal nature presupposes that one considers the text as a collection of ready-made prescriptions applicable in all circumstances. The Qur'an, like any written text, and particularly texts associated with the foundations of a religion, is open to a limitless number of interpretations, even in the case of verses which may appear clear.[27] Scholars specialising in the sources of jurisprudence did not, however, take account of the aims behind particular solutions figuring in the text of the Qur'an or of the context of individual verses that were the object of study.[28] While it is, of course, natural that the Qur'an be adopted as a reference and a guide by those striving to be authentic Muslims, believers need to be humble and prudent when dealing with the sacred text in order to avoid projecting onto the text subjective criteria and preferences inevitably affected by the prevailing environment. The written document enjoyed a quasi-sacred status among those scholars who imagined that their methodological research in the linguistic field would lead them to absolute truth, allowing them to pronounce that the same imperative form of the verb indicated on certain occasions an obligation and on other occasions a free choice. In reality they projected their personal preoccupations and criteria of judgment onto the text, making it say what, in fact, it did not say. This led them to different conclusions about two formulations involving the imperative: wine is forbidden because of the word "avoid!" and the drinker is duly punished, while "write!" in the case of "writing a debt" leaves Muslims to choose whether to make a written record of the debt or not.[29]

This flawed approach to the text of the Qur'an is particularly manifest when verses are separated from one other and isolated from their context, be it that of a particular *sūra* or in a number of *sūras*. Among the most flagrant examples of this is the interpretation of verse 3 of the *sūra al-Nisā'*. On the one hand, they have clearly manipulated the phrase by splitting the conditional phrase "If you fear that you will not act justly towards the orphans, marry such women as seem good to you, two, three, four" into two parts, in contravention of the most elementary rules of grammar and logic. Moreover, by authorising four wives in all cases, they took no account of the feelings of the women who were obliged to share their husbands with others, and other questions such as an age disparity between spouses, the social inequalities of which women were victims and the fate of children (and their education) in an atmosphere of conflict between wives. They ignored the many verses which are the basis for an ethic of marriage in a Qur'anic perspective: mutual trust between spouses; tenderness; compassion; kindness and justice.[30] They also ignored the real reason for the authorisation of polygamy, namely the fear of being unjust towards orphans, as well as the particular historical context of this decision.[31] An existing social practice was legitimised, and values defended which one can unhesitatingly qualify as being contrary to those of the Qur'an, supported only by consensus (a question which will be examined later in this chapter) and not by what is imagined to be a faithful application of the text. The question is not whether or not the Qur'an was considered one of the sources of legislation but how Muslims scholars and others used it as a reference, dealt with it and interpreted it. Was it interpreted in a way which conformed to its spirit and internal logic or one that went no further than a literal reading of a limited number of verses which were then interpreted in a subjective manner? Scholars may have thought (or so they claimed) that they were faithfully transmitting the will and the wisdom of God Himself.

The second source of *fiqh* is the *Sunna* transmitted through *hadīth*. In the chapter of the *Muqadimmah* dealing with *hadīth* sciences, Ibn Khaldoun relates that "it is said that the number of traditions that Abū Hanīfa (d. 150/767) transmitted came to only seventeen or so. Mālik (d. 179/795) accepted as sound only the traditions found in the *Muwatta'*. They are at most only three hundred or so. Ahmad ibn Hanbal (d. 241/855) has 30,000 traditions in his *Musnad*. Ibn Hanbal said of the *Musnad* "In this book I have chosen from among 750,000 *hadīth*".[32] Ibn Khaldoun made this ostensibly simple observation in his role as an historian. Its significance generally goes unnoticed by the defenders of *Sunna* and *hadīth*. It is of little concern to us that Ibn Khaldoun evades the question of the enormous quantitative variation between the two imāms in the number of authentic traditions, merely repeating what Muslims held to be true since the *ahl al-hadīth* ("people of *hadīth*") had imposed their viewpoint on the community as a whole. One should note the prodigious proliferation in the number of traditions judged "authentic" in the period extending from the first half of the second century of the Hijra to the first half of the third century: from seventeen to 30,000 or 40,000. These figures alone should give grounds for doubting the authenticity of traditions attributed to the Prophet, when all of these are transmitted by a relatively small number of individuals.[33] Invention reached such proportions that the work carried out by al-Bukhāri, Muslim and other authors of the *hadīth* collections of the third century of the Hijra was in vain. In reality recourse to *hadīth* was necessary for the continuation of the activities of the *fuqahā*, and when Shāfi'ī (d. 204/819) did his utmost to give *Sunna* a solid foundation, he was in reality defending a particular vision of social order to which religion could give a necessary legitimacy. The Qur'an could do this only in a very limited way, whereas *hadīth* fulfilled this role through its capacity to generate a kind of unconscious collective fervour.

Only a handful of scholars challenged this manner of proceeding, but they were swamped by the dominant tendency, and it is unknown if they left any written documents. Little is known of them as individuals, nor do we have any idea of their number and importance. The most conclusive evidence for their existence is contained in a reference in the chapter Jimā 'al 'ilm in Shāfi'ī's *al-Umm*. Shāfi'ī quotes this person, "a distinguished scholar in his school", as having said:

Concerning something that God has commanded, how can you say on one occasion that it is a universal obligation, and on another that it is limited. You say that the divine command entails an obligation, while on another occasion it is merely an indication, or even that it indicates an authorisation. Very often, these different appreciations come from a *hadīth* which you have received from such and such a person, according to another, according to another, or from two or three *hadīths*, going back finally to the Prophet himself. As for those transmitters of *hadīth* you put forward as being of sound memory and authenticity you underline, I see that you and those who belong to your school of thought do not excuse any of those transmitters of *hadīth* of error, forgetfulness, or error in their *hadīth*. I see that you say, in the case of a number of them, that 'Such and such a scholar made a mistake in this or that *hadīth*.' And when someone challenges you about a *hadīth* known only to the specialists on the grounds that the Prophet did not actually say what is contained in the *hadīth*, and that therefore you (or those who informed you) were in error, I have seen that you do not ask him to repent but merely say to him: "What you have said is evil!" Is it permissible to distinguish between the precepts of the Qur'an when its meaning is evident for those who hearing it on the basis of information received from individuals? And we have seen how you describe them! Have you the right to put their remarks in the place of the Book of God, using them to give and to refuse?

Shāfi'ī, quoting this objector, continues:

If you persist in accepting their traditions with all the defects that you have evoked, what argument can you use against the person who refuses them? I accept nothing if there is the possibility of error therein; I accept only that of which I bear witness before God as I bear witness to the truth of his book of which no one can doubt a single word. No one can claim an exhaustive knowledge that he does not possess.[34]

It is not surprising that Shāfi'ī, having replied at length to the objection presented here in a summarised form, considers that refusal to accept a tradition when the Book of God is clear "is an opinion whose consequences are grave indeed". The objector declared: "The person who carries out a gesture that can be called prayer or the minimum act qualifying as *zakāt* (charity) has fulfilled the obligation without taking account of the time, even if he only made two prostrations each day. Where the Book of God has not clearly laid down a rule, there is no obligation involved."

This contestation of the *Sunna* had very little chance of developing. It was radically opposed to the prevailing orientation toward, on the one hand, a strict imposition of pre-Islamic mentalities, and an exaggeration of the role of the Prophet at the expense of his message, on the other hand. This orientation was influenced by popular mentality which sought a material expression of religious faith and the Prophet represented an historical figure with whom believers could identify. Words and deeds were attributed to the Prophet which, for the most part, reveal preoccupations unconnected with the personality of the Prophet as it is revealed in the most trustworthy source, namely the text of the Qur'an, and quite foreign to the simple and spontaneous spirit of the Prophet's time. They were the product of conflicts and challenges arising as the territory controlled by the Muslims expanded and the number of believers increased. Discord developed for political and other reasons. The historical context in which *fiqh* and its components developed made it virtually impossible to avoid strife between the main Muslim tendencies, especially the Shī'ites, the Khārijites and those who would come to be known as "the people of the Sunna and the Community". Each of these had their own chains of transmitters with the Shī'ites relying only on their imāms and the Khārijites imposing rigorous conditions for the authenticity of transmitters and generally accepted only *hadīth* transmitted by their own scholars while criticising those of the Sunnis:

> We see these specialists in *hadīth* criticising one of the *hadīth* transmitters for a trifling reasons, then go on, despite their knowledge of these attacks, to accept the traditions of the Companions and accept the versions of the person who rebukes as well as that of the person who is rebuked. This is nothing to do with religion. These specialists kow-tow to whoever holds power and are slaves of whoever is stronger. They hand down *hadīth* which favour the rulers of their country, and transfer their allegiance elsewhere when those rulers fall from power.[35]

On the other hand, Sunni scholars reject the traditions of their adversaries, whom they describe as being "subjected to passion and innovation".

It is noteworthy that the dispute about the transmission, as in similar cases in the field of *fiqh*, did not put in question the text of the *hadīth* except concerning questions which divided the community, such as the imamate. This consensus brought together members of the factions and schools despite the rivalries and conflicts in other areas. They shared the same bases and methods for their reflection, although their positions were far removed from the aspirations of the Prophetic message, which strove to give religious reflection an orientation based on a blend of gratuitous divine love and human obedience and responsibility. Obedience did not exclude divine gratuity and human responsibility.

The research undertaken by the specialists in *usūl al-fiqh* for authoritative texts did not always produce positive results. The first generation of Muslims did not undertake such a quest, considering it unnecessary. The development of urban life as conditions stabilised in the conquered territories, new ways of working, and concomitant transformations in an evermore complex way of life brought about legal situations requiring legislation for which there were no precedents at the time of the Prophet or in the period immediately following. This is what led to consensus (*ijmāʿ*) becoming the third basis for legislation, in the absence of a text.[36] The specialists in *usūl al-fiqh* made great efforts to produce textual support for this source, realising that the verses relied upon by certain scholars required a degree of manipulation in order to constitute decisive proof. The *hadīth* mobilised to this end were more pertinent to the needs of the community than they were to the question of consensus on a particular judgment about a question for which there was no text in the Qurʾan or in *Sunna*. These *hadīth* were inferior to the *hadīth mutawātir* supported by multiple *isnāds* (lines of transmission) which guarantee certitude according to the criteria of the specialists in *hadīth* and *usūl al-fiqh*.[37] The end result is a circular argument according to which consensus is the only authentic basis for consensus. Ghazāli, fully aware of this impasse to which he alluded in the *Mustasfā*, thought that it could be solved through use of the concept of "custom", but the difficulty was not resolved in this way. Despite its somewhat scanty legitimacy, consensus continued to be considered the "origin of origins", while the Hanbalite Ibn ʿAqīl (d. 513/1119) gave it precedence over the text:

> It is a degree surer than the text, as the text, even if it is the word of an infallible person, can be replaced by another text which contradicts and abrogates it. Consensus, on the other hand, cannot err, safe from contradiction or abrogation, since there is nothing similar to it which can prevail over it.[38]

Whatever the difficulties arising from such claims, it is opportune to recall that consensus is one of the mainstays of Judaism and Christianity, although under different names. Institutional religions certainly need some kind of consensus as otherwise it is difficult to demonstrate the solidity of unified doctrine, liturgy and ethics which religious authorities try to impose on the community of believers. The move toward making consensus one of the foundations of *fiqh* encountered opposition later qualified as "deviance" as *Sunna* became an established cultural entity. It is likely that al-Naẓẓām (d. 230/844) was not the only person to reject the consensus, as all the *uṣūl* texts say, quoting one another, although the details of his and his companions' arguments are unknown. Was it because of the practical impossibility of arriving at such a consensus, or because of its fragility as a reference, or some other reason?[39] Two points may be noted:

First, the premises of the *uṣūl* specialists are far removed from their conclusions. Their starting point is the consensus of the Islamic community as a whole, illustrated (according to their interpretation) by the following verse: (Sūra 2:143): "Thus We appointed you a midmost nation that you might be witnesses to the people and the Messenger might be a witness to you." They conclude by saying that the only valid consensus is that of the experts in interpretation, to the exclusion of all others, especially the common people and those whose opinion is of little worth, let alone women and slaves.[40] Certain subjects have been monopolised by those who consider that they speak in God's name and know what He commands and what He forbids. In the words of one scholar: "These are matters understood by the scholars alone and have not been entrusted to others."[41] This is a blatant form of marginalisation, exercised against the majority of the Muslim community, considered as minors in need of a tutor, a practice entirely contrary to the spirit of the Prophet's message which makes not the slightest allusion to this kind of elitism. The message of the Prophet is addressed to all people and to all believers without distinction. This was one of the main reasons why the leaders of the Quraysh initially did not believe the preaching of Muhammad and refused to follow him: "When it is said to them: 'believe as the people believe', they say, 'Shall we believe as fools believe?'" (Sūra 2:13).[42]

The second observation would be that consensus could be a force for innovation and adaptation to changing circumstances if it were based on democratic principles and corresponded to the aspirations of the majority of people in quotidian concerns, such as food, dress, economic relations and ethics. What has, in fact, happened is that the consensus of a particular period in history, that of the *fuqahāʾ* in the second/eighth and third/ninth centuries, has been considered binding for all time, along with the myriad detailed conditions attached by the *uṣūl* specialists from the fifth/eleventh century onwards, when this branch of learning was formally organised. The solutions adopted at a particular point in time, that of the rightly-guided (*rāshidūn*) caliphs, the Companions and the chief Followers, were made into an unchangeable set of founding precepts. It might have been possible in so doing to retain the relative spontaneity and flexibility of the period instead of sanctifying the past, a past which the 'ulamā' who codified *fiqh* imagined to have been a period of perfect uniformity within the Muslim community. They camouflaged the rich variety which existed in reality, where differences of opinion coexisted with concord and harmony. At times, those in authority imposed their point of view, while at other moments in history heated debate took place and scholars competed in good faith as they sought truth. As in all human history, qualities and defects were interwoven. Although the *hadīth* "What Muslims approve, God approves" only appears in the *Musnad* of Ibn Hanbal, and its authenticity is questionable, it is worthy of being adopted as a factor of Muslim unity in the face of trials or imminent danger.[43] In other circumstances diversity is desirable, and one should take into account the opinion of the community at a particular point in time, be it in conformity with tradition or not, especially when the circumstances and situations of consensus have undergone radical change.

The same causes tend to produce the same effects and the multiplication of "cases" for which it was not possible to find a text or obtain a consensus led to analogy or *qiyās* being made the fourth basis for legislation. "For everything that befalls a Muslim there is a statute applicable or there is an indication of the way of truth": this is the famous expression of Shāfi'ī.[44] There are grounds for contesting this axiom which is far removed from the spirit and letter of the Qur'an: the evaluation of human acts may vary in function of historical factors, while religion should not pass judgment on appearances which sometimes do not reflect interior attitudes. Human responsibility means pursuing evolving ideals, with the aim of reconciling individual freedom and the higher interests of the community. This point of view may seem self-evident to a modern mentality, but its adoption fatally undermines the foundations of *fiqh* along with the process of reasoning by analogy. This method does not always provide a stable foundation for a "branch" of *fiqh* in need of a statute, because once such a statute has been found it becomes in its turn a fixed basis for the practice of analogy. The decisions of the *fuqahā'* are not based on a uniform pattern of logic, an observation made long ago by those opposed to analogical reasoning. Analogy, they noted, cannot be applied in the case of *furūdh*: all the legal schools require that women fast to make up for the fasting they missed during Ramadhan because of their periods, although they do not require that she make up for prayers missed for the same reason. No logical or rational explanation is given for this.[45]

Reliance on analogy produced a backward-looking mentality insufficiently focused on the present, let alone the future. The present, however, with its values and factional interests influences the way that the past is understood: analogy (*qiyās*) is far from being a neutral operation, and takes insufficient account of the intentions of the message of Islam. Analogical reasoning is fundamentally flawed, as the *fuqahā*' who use it, particularly in recent times, do not recognise that its justifications are purely formal, believing that through it they express the will of God. In other words, the preoccupation in the field of *qiyās* (as in other areas) with proving the continuity of practice between the time of the Prophet and other periods had a number of dangerous consequences:

> it failed to achieve the ultimate objective of every legislative system, namely justice, which presupposes freedom and individual reponsibility;[46]

> it claimed (a claim which does not stand up to critical historical examination or objective consideration) that analogy is an expression of divine, rather than human judgment in the cases in which it is the deciding factor; and

> it closed off access to the revealed text for those who wish to encounter it directly without having to use the *fuqahā*' and exegetes as intermediaries.[47]

Usūl al fiqh underwent no real evolution since the work of scholars, such as Abu al Husain al Basri (d. 436/1044), author of the *Mu'tamid*, Imām al-Haramain al Juwaini (d. 478/1085), author of the *Burhān*, Ibn Hazm (d. 456/1063), author of the *Ihkām*, al-Ghazāli (d. 505/1111), author of the *al-Mustasfa*, and Fakhr al-dīn al-Rāzi (d. 606/1209). Subsequent authors depended on them, merely exposing, summing up, or defending the point of view of the school to which they belonged. Hanefite scholars, for example, put forward the theory of tacit consensus, in contrast to other schools of *fiqh*. Scholars also defended secondary elements of *usūl al fiqh* accepted by certain schools, including personal interpretation (*istihsān*), the presumption of continued exercise of a right (*istishāb*), rights deriving from custom and the public interest (*masālih mursala*). Abu Ishāq al-Shātibi (538/1144–590/1194) attempted to take into account not only questions of terminology but also the ultimate aims of Islamic law in his *Muwāfaqāt*, a work that stands apart from the rest. There were, however, no other scholars able to continue this approach and remove the vestiges of the ossified mentality of the *usūl al fiqh* specialists. Muhammad al Tāhir Ben Achour and Allāl al-Fāsi (1329/1910–1393/1974) were aware of the challenges and adumbrated possible solutions, although their work does not really represent a clearly formulated and complete break with prevailing approaches in the area of *usūl al fiqh*, which even today continues to repeat traditional discourse in social and intellectual context transformed out of all recognition.[48] Recent work can even be said to more superficial than the great works of past scholars, who had a better grasp of the questions studied.[49]

Qur'anic Exegesis *(tafsīr)*

Qur'anic exegesis cannot, of course, be separated from other branches of Islamic learning. It, too, gradually became an independent field of study, with *fuqahā'*, specialists in the foundations of religious law, theologians, *hadīth* specialists, historians and linguists all working in this area. These specialities were complementary and interconnected, and scholars shared values and a way of looking at the world and approached religious questions in similar ways. All believed the Qur'an to be a legislative text whose prescriptions were valid across frontiers of space and time. None of them imagined that the message of the Prophet was one intended to liberate people from the servile imitation of their ancestors (even though they were considered the pious founding fathers) and guide their conduct in society, encouraging them to act responsibly. This message frees believers from the danger of alienation, as God is only absolute and all other cultural phenomena belong to the domain of human history and are, therefore, relative, prone to change and subject to criticism and analysis. They can be improved or amended.

We have emphasised the fundamental characteristics of Qur'anic exegesis (which are also present in other areas of Islamic thought), in order to demonstrate that there is a clear distinction between the essence of the message of Islam and its application. The preoccupations of the founding generations of Islam are equally remote from those of contemporary Muslims. We do not wish to denigrate the scholarly endeavours of the past, to which today's Muslims are indebted, but simply to demonstrate that the solutions they elaborated to questions confronting them were valid for their time. These solutions were connected to the context in which they lived, one very different from that in which we and our contemporaries live, whatever their race, language, religion, way of thinking and civilisation. This recognition of change and evolution runs contrary to the natural human tendency to cling to what is familiar, and which resists novelty and innovation. Religion has in the past been a guarantee against chaos and has been an irreplaceable source of legitimacy for social institutions. It is difficult to imagine how they could be considered legitimate without the legitimacy conferred by religion. Religion is not responsible for this course of events, but it can be made to play this role more efficiently than other highly fragile sources of legitimacy. Life is itself an uncertain balance of conflicting elements and if this takes on a fixed, unchanging form, death is imminent. It is no surprise then that people should endeavour to forget this tragic condition by searching for stability: they seek solace in religion under the illusion that religion can guarantee this stability. At the same time they overlook the price that has to be paid for this sense of security, one that is authentic and false at the same time. Is there a higher price to be paid than that of renouncing the challenge of facing reality, and losing that which is most distinctively human: freedom and responsibility, without which humans sink to the level of animals?

The traditional view that Muslims have of *tafsīr* is an idealistic one.[50] Since the message of Islam was seen by many as having a legislative character, people believed that the Prophet explained to his contemporaries the more obscure aspects of the Qur'an's prescriptions. The Companions were, therefore, better equipped than other believers after the death of the Prophet to elucidate obscure verses or general dispositions which were not set out in detail. However, did the Prophet really have to explain the revelation? Its content was sufficiently clear and generally relevant to the context in which the Companions lived. Muslims came to believe with time, and as their way of life began to change, that the Qur'an alone was insufficient to provide the solutions required by an institutionalised religion. They, therefore, ascribed to the Prophet and Companions the capacities to compensate for this lack, justifying through the prophetic *hadīth* the imitation of the Companions ("my companions are as stars: imitate them and be guided by them" etc.), then that of the Followers and preceding generations in general. This was especially the case when a significant group of Muslims, from the fourth/eleventh century onwards and in periods of decline, considered that the glories of Muslim civilisation were waning ("The best century is mine, then those following it"). There was a deeply-felt desire to return to the origins of faith and culture, seen as a golden age of plenitude and perfection.[51]

Qur'anic exegesis was necessary to determine how religious rites should be accomplished, and also to give detailed accounts of prophets and ancient peoples presented by the Qur'an in a summary fashion. In the case of the former, the Qur'an deliberately avoided going into details, and succinct verses were explained by relying on *Sunna* in its lived-out dimension, the ritual practices which gradually became formalised over time. Subsequently, *hadīth* describing the deeds and directives of the prophets were recounted, and it was decided that the Prophet's example should be followed. With regard to the stories of the prophets, the practice was to consult the "people of the book" who had become Muslims, such Ka'b al-Ahbār and Wahb ibn Munabbih who were familiar with the sacred texts of the Jews and Christians, or at least the oral traditions circulating in their milieu which were a mixture of historical and marvellous elements. This led to the inclusion in Qur'anic exegesis of what are known as the *israiliyyāt*, whose fabulous character has left a lasting imprint on *tafsīr*, one that will persist if modern historical science is not better employed to help commentators distinguish between the style of these stories (which reflect the state of learning at the time of the Prophet and the first generation of commentators) on the one hand, and the aim of exegesis, on the other hand, namely, to guide following generations of Muslims in their reflection and discernment.

At the beginning of the second/eighth century, when *fiqh* became an autonomous science and theology developed its rational and textual enquiries, scholars began to search in the Qur'an for justifications for juridical provisions related to socio-economic questions, and for textual support and guidance in the difficult questions beginning to trouble believers: divine justice and the existence of evil; the extent of human freedom; justice in the world to come and so on. Each legal school, each group of theologians, projected onto the text the views of their leaders, along with the opinions and beliefs they expressed. Certain verses were considered clear and precise while others were abrogated or ambiguous. The exegetes did not, however, take into account the essential difference between the nature of the discourse of revelation which relies on symbol and metaphor and the conceptual discourse which characterises human science in general. Exegetical texts became the obligatory means of access to the text of the Qur'an, and these secondary texts impeded direct understanding of the text and free personal reflection. Exegetical research was accompanied by linguistic explanations of the text, be they lexicological, grammatical, syntactical, or rhetorical, justifying rather than serving as a basis for the various texts that were selected, despite their disparate and even contradictory nature. The interest of

al-Zamkhshari (d. 538/1143) in the language did not prevent him from using the
Qur'an to defend his own Mu'tazilite point of view, as did his contemporaries
Tabari (d. 310/922) and Rāzi (d. 606/1209) (in the Sunni camp), or the Shī'ites
Tūsi (d. 460/1067) and Tabari (d. 548/1153). If it is the case that the text can
take on meaning only in the light of the rules of discourse and language, then
a written text has multiple meanings which reflect the expectations of a reader
in particular circumstances. The Qur'an, as Ali Ibn Abī Tālib said, does not
speak of itself, it is men who speak through it. The aim of *tafsīr* was, therefore, to
enclose the text in a zeriba of interpretations approved by the theological current
or school of jurisprudence to which exegetical writers belonged. The door was
closed to free research untrammelled by time honoured controversy, despite
tafsīr being considered to be a science which no one could claim to have brought
to its final stage of development. These two factors may explain why successive
generations of Muslims compiled works of *tafsīr* which leave the reader with an
impression of the same subject-matter being treated by one author after another,
who merely fall into line or tinker with already existing points of view. Ever since
tafsīr became an independent art or craft (*sinā'ā*) all the exegetes have felt duty
bound to follow the sūra and verses in the order of the *mushaf* one after the other,
limiting themselves (or being compelled to do so by outside circumstances) to
the juxtaposition of different opinions instead of following a different approach
which would have brought them, through personal reflection, to discover the
aims and main themes of the Qur'anic texts.

Prior to embarking on this kind of intellectual enterprise, scholars needed to
be knowledgeable in the sciences of the Qur'an, to ensure that deductions were
not made on an unsound basis. It is unsurprising that many volumes of exegesis
are incomplete, as their authors died before completing them. Along with the
history of the text, language sciences and the *qirā'āt*, volumes of *tafsīr* contain
the *israiliyyāt*, incoherent traditions, the ponderous considerations of the *fuqahā'*
as well as traditions whose origins are in popular, oral culture.[52] The overall aim
of the Qur'an is swamped by these disparate elements, and the text becomes a
pretext or an occasion to defend values tenuously connected with the Qur'an
and which are often undesirable. Tabari hesitates between fideism and humility
before the Word of God, between speaking in the name of God, on the one
hand, and giving his own interpretation after the verse: "God, may His Name be
exalted" (or some similar expression) says ..., or suggesting what seems to Him to
be the probable meaning of the verse: "According to me, the nearest to the truth

is ..." (or some similar expression), on the other hand. The former approach is the one that came to dominate *tafsīr* after Tabari, marked by an exaggerated fideism and the rejection of everything the exegete considers alien to his options and those of his school of thought.

In reality certain leading exegetes, particularly Rāzi, were broad-minded. Far from remaining silent about the difficulties they encountered, they set them out clearly and tried to surmount them insofar as possible, examining the question from different points of view, bringing to bear the full weight of their culture and learning. If they failed to find a convincing solution, they left the matter in God's hands and recognised their inability. They were influenced by a deeply-rooted cultural tradition which prevented them from directly engaging with the text, unencumbered by the interpretative baggage of previous generations.[53] In other words, *tafsīr* was a complete structure from which no element could be withdrawn without the whole structure trembling. This explains the resistance of the representatives of traditional culture to any position which diverged from tradition. They were unaware that this tradition existed within history and that it was linked to situations and values far removed from those of present-day Muslims. This is why a renewal of Qur'anic exegesis is needed, taking account of the results of human sciences, and with different premises from those of the defenders of the traditional system, which has become a burden for Islamic thought.

Hadīth

The problems associated with *hadīth* have already been discussed, in particular the fact that *Sunna* was considered one of the sources of *fiqh*. It will be dealt with here simply as one of the essential elements of the Islamic sciences. Rarely is there such a difference between the linguistic and the technical sense of a word as there is in the case of *hadīth* and *Sunna*. Their meaning has evolved and they have come to designate the same object or two very similar ones. They are used indifferently to indicate the words, deeds and decisions of the Prophet, in the form fixed by the *hadīth* collections approved by the Sunnis and codified in the third/ninth century.[54]

Hadīth infringes the Prophet's command that only the Qur'an was to be written down, a command that strips *hadīth* of its legitimacy and leaves the Qur'an as the guiding light for Muslims in this world and the next. The Prophet's personal declarations were not to be normative or obligatory. Muslims had exactly opposing aspirations. The radically new nature of their vocation and their lack of preparedness to take on the organisation of their lives as believers prevented them from heeding the Prophet's invitation. The first generation of Muslims doubtless heeded the Prophet's invitation not to record what they may have heard him say. The rare individuals who recorded in a scattered fashion the words of the Prophet which they heard from the Companions wanted to keep what they heard for their own spiritual nourishment rather than diffusing it around them. It is not by chance that this principle was transgressed by the caliph, 'Umar ibn 'Abd al'Aziz at the beginning of the second/eighth century, the caliph remembered by the Muslim community as the fifth of the rightly-guided (*rashidūn*) caliphs. He needed to produce a symbol of virtue and piety in order to have a chance of being accepted. According to the Sunnis, it was al-Zuhri who took upon himself the codification, opening the door through which would stream reliable transmitters of *hadīth* and fabricators alike.

Hadīth began to be codified at the same time as other branches of learning, pre-Islamic poetry in particular. This poetry was the basis chosen by linguistic scholars for the collecting together of the different elements of the Arabic language and for laying down rules for the language. This poetry naturally contained rare terms and unfamiliar constructions requiring explanation, in the same way that numerous Qur'anic terms required a commentary. It is striking that the scholars of the second/eighth century did not consider *hadīth* as a proof, and they did not use it to lay down rules or for commentary and explanation, despite their insistence on the eloquence of the Prophet. They were unsure whether statements attributed to him had been narrated in the very words of the Prophet or simply in a way which preserved their general meaning. The *hadīth* were collected together more than a century after the time of the Prophet. In addition, the non-Arab *mawāli* (clients) formed the majority of transmitters of *hadīth*. Why should the faithful believe in *hadīths* whose number grew daily, with invention and falsification rife? The spread of *hadīth* falsification was, therefore, a sufficient reason to doubt their authenticity. It was also one of the elements which stimulated the zealous quest of the *hadīth* collectors, when their compilations gradually took on a degree of sacredness approaching that of the Qur'an itself to the extent that the expression "recounted by the two sheikhs" (al-Bukhāri and Muslim) was sufficient to validate a *hadīth* and make it binding. The imām Mālik had little need, in the context of the Hejaz in the west of the Arabian peninsula, to invent *hadīth*. His *Muwatta'* contains only around 300 *hadīth*, and was considered the most reliable book after the book of God Himself. Bukhāri, Muslim and the authors of *hadīth* compilations in the third/ninth century followed a different method, selecting as authentic according to their criteria only a very small number of the *hadīth* which had come down to them. The Shī'ite *hadīth* collections of the fourth/tenth century likewise followed their own methods of authentication, as the only valid line of transmission is that of the imāms, even if the divergences between these collections and the Sunni collections concerned only a limited number of cases.

The criteria of authenticity were not sufficiently established at the time of the compilation of the *hadīth* collections for scholars to apply them automatically; scholars had to search for these criteria without being able to rely on precedents. All the available evidence seems to show that they were models of honesty, rectitude and abnegation, seeking only the rewards of the world to come. They shied away from any criticism of the content of traditions attributed to the Prophet or of the form of these traditions, and were likewise reluctant to express a personal opinion about the information contained in the *hadīth*. They, there-fore, concentrated on the chain of transmitters rather than on the text itself, to establish the authenticity of the mass of *hadīth* they had laboriously gathered together or about which they had learned in various ways

Hadīth scholars stipulated that for a *hadīth* to be acceptable, it needed to fulfil the following conditions. The chain of transmitters would be composed of specific individuals who could be identified clearly and not simply by a name, a vague surname, or an epithet. Each transmitter also had to have been of an age which allowed him to have recognised the person he claims to have met and whose statement he transmitted. At the very least, grounds should exist for supposing that such a meeting took place. They also stipulated that transmitters be reputed for their capacities for memorising, their precision and their clarity. Among other conditions they set out were the need for the transmitter of *hadīth* to be of honourable character, with nothing in his conduct which detracted from his standing as a man of virtue and honour, qualities grouped under the heading of *al-murū'a*.[55] Nor was he to be associated with dubious innovators and impetuous hotheads. In this way the criteria for authenticating the chain of transmission gradually took form, and became the main preoccupation of the *hadīth* collectors under the name of "the science of invalidation and declaration of credibility" (*'ilm al jarh wa-l-t'adīl*). Initially *hadīth* collectors did not accord great importance to the ways in which traditions were transmitted, although the exigencies of research led scholars to give greater attention to this. They distinguished between various categories, according to whether the *hadīth* could be traced back to the Prophet, to a Companion quoting the Prophet directly, or to another person quoting the words of a Companion. *Hadīth* which had only one transmitter were differentiated from those which had several transmitters. Other categories included *hadīth* read in the presence of a sheikh who verified the authenticity of the text containing the *hadīth*, as distinct from a *hadīth* recounted by a sheikh relying on his memory alone. Yet another category included copies of *hadīth* entrusted by the sheikh to his student, with or without permission to transmit it. These are some of the categories which gradually fixed technical terms, the difference between which could be understood only by scholars practised in this arcane science, able to grasp the difference between "he informed me" and "he informed us", between "he told me" and "he told us", between "according to someone" and "I heard from someone" or "I read in the presence of someone". Each of these ways of transmission has a corresponding grade: the *hadīth* can be valid, accurate, good, weak, isolated among other qualifications. The implicit aim of the classification was for scholars to give preference to the *hadīth* transmitted by the school to which they belonged.

The meticulous research involved in *hadīth* studies demonstrates that the question of the authenticity of prophetic *hadīth* was a dilemma for early scholars.[56] Ibn Qutayba (d. 276/889), in his treatise entitled *ta'wīl mukhtalif al-hadīth*[57] dating from shortly after the period of collection and compilation, shows that scholarly concern with formal aspects of *hadīth* masked contradictory, irrational, and counter-Qur'anic elements in the *hadīth* corpus, couched in mediocre and outlandish language. All this reveals the extent to which *hadīth* were falsified, credible only on the basis of arbitrary interpretation. Faced with these discrepancies, a small number of 'ulamā' belonging to later generations attempted to harmonise the different versions. Al-Māzāri (d. 536/1141), al-Nawawī (d. 676/1277), al-'Asqalānī (d. 852/1448), and al-Qastallānī (d. 923/1517) set about commenting on the different collections, making tremendous efforts to defend their coherence and present them in a way which conformed to established dogmas, prescriptions and opinion. To do this they drew on all their linguistic and historical knowledge.

In the light of these observations, the following three significant conclusions may be noted.

First, the field of *hadīth* study is considered one of the sciences which are part of the Muslim heritage. Reason has no role to play, and individual believers have merely to assent to *hadīth* which the Muslim community has agreed to accept. Approved traditions were in reality those acceptable to a particular scholarly faction which had carried the day for reasons unconnected with the value and significance of the *hadīth* which were adopted. Collecting and classifying involved selection, which meant retaining certain elements and eliminating others. This can happen only by applying methods of rational criticism to *hadīth*, even if specialists maintain that only the chain of transmission will be critically examined.[58] The corpus finally retained reflects the community's representation of the Prophet after the period of revelation, against a background of radical change. *Hadīth* collections also mirror prevailing values among *hadīth* scholars, as distinct from scholars in other fields.

Secondly, the contents of *hadīth* collections are constituted for the most part of traditions transmitted by a single scholar (*ahād*), and are not limited to the words and deeds attributed to the Prophet. Words and deeds of the Companions were also included, and they were accorded the same exemplary value as those of the Prophet. In addition, the definition of "Companion" was widened to include anyone who had seen the Prophet, even once. These persons then became the basis for a chain of transmission as did those who had in fact lived with the Prophet over a period of time, believed in him and attributed to him qualities of perfection and infallibility. The initial link in the chain of transmission cannot be criticised, unlike the other elements.

Thirdly, *hadīth* was treated in the same way as the Qur'an and was considered of equal rank. Believers clung to the literal meaning of traditions, memorised them, read them without due reflection and celebrated the completion of study in this field. Consequently, *hadīth* was a subject of research in the field of *fiqh* in the same way as the Qur'an: questions examined included abrogation, the particular and the general, what was implicit or explicit, absolute and restricted, as well as other traditional research in the field of Qur'anic science. Scholars were insufficiently prudent, given the context in which *hadīth* were codified. One might imagine that these elements taken together mean that the Muslim community's heritage of Prophetic *hadīth* is somehow valueless. Nothing could be further from the truth. *Hadīth* represents a storehouse of living piety, evoking noble and timeless aspirations. Its content is varied in quality, with values juxtaposed with others which are arid and lifeless. One finds vestiges of traditional values together with ideals which the passage of time has not eroded, and which remain valid in all circumstances. All this material needs to be examined and evaluated, in the light of the main thrust of the message of Islam. *Hadīth* should not be considered sacred or interpreted literally. If these requirements are met, *hadīth* will remain alive in the hearts of believers. Will Muslims rise to the challenges facing them?

*Theology (*kalām*)*

The interpenetration of *fiqh*, *tafsīr* and *hadīth*, on the one hand, and *kalām*, on the other hand, is largely responsible for the impasse in which the Islamic sciences find themselves. Since time immemorial Muslims have thought of theology as a system of rational apologetics. In the words of Ibn Khaldoun, in the chapter devoted to theology in the sixth chapter of the *Muqadimmah* "this is a science which involves arguing with logical proofs in defence of the articles of faith and refuting innovators who deviate in their dogmas from the early Muslims and Muslim orthodoxy".[59]

Such a definition leaves to one side, and even refutes, large swathes of theological reflection, in particular that undertaken by the Mu'tazilites. Elements of this have penetrated into Sunni, Ash'arite and Maturidite thought. Such a definition concentrates on the apologetic dimension of theology, where the eternal truths appear as a set of unchanging data which have merely to be defended, a vision far removed from historical reality. Contemporary researchers agree on the close link between the first attempts at systematic theological thought and the political realities prevailing after the "Great Schism", which saw a struggle for power and a conflict among the Companions for which the Muslim community was unprepared. Many questions were raised about what attitude believers should have toward the combatants, their victims and those who remained neutral. Could they all be in the right? If not, who was in error and who was right?

Against the background of these events which played a determining role in the development of the first attempts at theological reflection, the passage from spontaneous to rational faith was not accompanied by a process of reflection based only on Qur'anic verses dealing with themes such as destiny, the existence of evil in the world, sanctions in the next world and other questions with which theological reflection has to engage. Rational theological reflection could take form only through the prism of the community's culture, either that of their own native environment or that of neighbouring or rival cultures. Islamic theology developed by collecting together these elements and blending them with the data of the text. This needs to be borne in mind lest one be tempted to see *kalām* as an autonomous science, free from the constraints of time and space. *Kalām* did take on these characteristics, although only after methods, categories and logical processes developed which led to successive theses being elaborated. The debate surrounding them made its mark on the solutions destined to be propagated and diffused. This is at the heart of the commonly held idea that true belief existed among the members of the first generations of Muslims before the appearance of doubts and innovations through capriciousness and error. Sunni doctrine had, however, emerged from conflict between rival interpretations, and it can be said to owe its existence to them. Some of these interpretations were retained while others were rejected for a variety of factors, which led to the ultimate triumph of one faction over another. Ibn Khaldoun, in considering that theology is not necessary at the present time for the scholar since heretics and innovators have disappeared, demonstrates that he has fallen victim to the complacent mentality of his time which considered theological reflection super-fluous. This was thought to be a positive development: in reality it is a sign of the immobility that sets in before death ensues.

This means that apologetics, which characterised *kalām* in its later stages, stands in the way of its primary and fundamental task of understanding and expounding divine revelation, not by an indiscriminate reliance on the opinions of previous scholars but by letting each generation exploit the learning available to them, whether or not this runs counter to traditional beliefs. This is the only way to be convinced of one's beliefs, and to be a convincing witness to them. For this reason philosophy, history, sociology, psychology and linguistics, along with other disciplines should not be competitors or handmaidens of theology. Each of them has its particular field, methods, premises and conclusions. It is in the theologian's interest to follow modern learning and exploit it to the best lest a gap open up between theology and contemporary science, making theolog-ical language incomprehensible even if theologians have committed their learning to memory and can repeat it, parrot-like, to perfection.[60] Theologians must revise in particular learning that has become obsolete and fallen behind contemporary intellectual development. Jāhiz (*c.* 160–255/*c.* 776–868) long ago observed:

> The theologian can only muster a unified knowledge of *kalām* and master this art as leader of a school by being equally competent in theology

and philosophy. The scholar is the person who is knowledgeable in both subjects.[61]

Here, as elsewhere in this book, the history of theology or the other Islamic sciences will not be set out in detail; rather these disciplines will be examined to see to what extent they are in keeping with the spirit of the message of the Prophet as it has been presented here. Three main characteristics should be noted: first, theology as developed in the work of scholars of various schools is not simply an Islamic science but is of Greco-Islamic character. The theologians, to quote the *qādī* Abd al-Jabbār, "studied only that which aided the victory of monotheism and divine justice", although to attain this aim they used the categories and logic of Greek philosophy.[62] One should not imagine that the intellectual instrument employed is innocent or neutral: in reality it influences the content of the science in question, orientating it in a direction different from that which it would have taken had another instrument been used. *Hadith* specialists realised this along with all those who rejected philosophy and refused to adapt its concepts to the religious faith of the first generation of Muslims. It goes without saying that the logic of the Greeks and other peoples of antiquity differed from modern logic. Traditional logic was linked in particular to mathematical science which has progressed over the last two centuries in a prodigious manner, to the extent that this traditional logic is no longer valid. The same can be said of numerous categories and philosophical terms used by scholars studying divinity, prophethood, the world to come, among other subjects which seem religious or merely Islamic in character. These categories and terms, borrowed from the physics, astronomy and geography of a thousand years ago, reflect a bygone age and are of historical and documentary interest only. These categories and terms were intended to render the language of belief in conceptual terms comprehensible to cultivated Muslims in the first centuries. They were reduced to mere rote learning and repetition in an age of intellectual stagnation.

The second characteristic of theology from its beginnings was a tendency for debates to become inflexible when the subjects under discussion should have been examined with prudence and humility. Divergence of opinions often led to mutual exclusion and accusations of unbelief and heresy. Theologians generally sought to crush their opponents by bombarding them with arguments without examining how valid or erroneous their own positions were, or if they were contradictory or inaccurate. Abu Hanifa, summing up the situation at his time (before it deteriorated further) said:

> We looked at one another in silence, fearing that our companions would make an error. You too look at one another and want your companion to make a mistake. He who wants to see his companion stumble wants to call him an unbeliever: the person who wants to call his companion an unbeliever is perhaps an unbeliever himself.[63]

Those who rejected *kalām,* in particular the *hadīth* specialists who described the Mu'tazalites and theologians in general as dangerous innovators, were as inflexible as their opponents. Ibn Hanbal, for example, states with complete self-assurance:

> These are the teachings of people of learning and influence ... anyone who contradicts or criticises these teachings or reproves those who propound them is a dangerous innovator, he is excluded from the community, he has strayed from the way of Sunna and truth.[64]

In general, exaggerated fideism and dogmatism[65] were dominant, leaving no room for personal research since truth was seen as ready-made: Muslims had only to discover it. Truth was behind or above believers, not in front of them.

The third characteristic feature of *kalām* is its relation to politics. Certain members of the first generation of theologians, such as Ghaylān al-Dimashqi, Ja'd ibn Dirham and Jahm ibn Safwān paid with their lives for their opposition to the Ummayad regime.[66] Mu'tazilism enjoyed for a period the support of the Abbasids before falling into disfavour. The adherents of Asha'ari and al-Matūridi gave Sunni theology a defensive orientation from the fourth/tenth century onwards, concerned ostensibly with questions of doctrine. In reality, socio-political issues were the principal preoccupation of scholars. Servile submission was legitimised under the guise of obedience. Intentionally or not theologians, such as al-Bāqillāni (d. 403/1012), 'Abd al-Qāhir al-Baghdādi (d. 428/1036), al-Ghazāli (d. 505/1111) and their successors served the interests of existing structures of power. They consecrated the formula according to which each person is not the author of his or her acts, which constitutes a denial of the principle of causality. Otherwise limits were placed on divine omnipotence and the miracles of the prophets were denied. The doctrine of the Jabarites recalled the words of Mu'awiya when he took power, one of many justifications for tyranny and exploitation: "Had God not judged me fit to exercise this charge, He would not have given it to me. If God had found our situation undesirable, he would have changed it."[67] Generations of Muslims were educated in a way which led them to refuse any discernment in the different areas of life. Human acts were not attributed to natural, social or logical causes and the First (divine) Cause was immediately identified in questions both anodyne and momentous. Ignorance was thought to be a sign and condition of piety, an attitude which favoured the spread of fatalism, charlatanry, oppression and fanaticism in many and varied forms.

Sufism

Theology was founded on reason, whereas Sufism is founded on sentiment. The position occupied by Sufism is similar to that of mysticism in other Eastern and Western religious traditions, both ancient and contemporary. From the third/ninth century onwards, conflict between religious law and wisdom, as well as between inner truth and law, preoccupied Muslim scholars. The history of Islamic thought saw many attempts to harmonise the claims of these rival disciplines. In the end philosophy was made into an independent discipline with only logic and physics being retained by theology. Some of the excesses of Sufism were corrected, leaving it free to cultivate interior spiritual life and examine the depths of the soul, on condition that it recognised, at least formally, the utility of external forms of religion and the need to respect them.

There is general agreement among Sufis that their experience cannot be expressed through language and for this reason they often use poetry, aphorisms and proverbs. Sufi literature is marked by symbols, allusions and evocations. Familiar expressions take on esoteric meanings and veiled significations. It is, therefore, difficult to evaluate this domain with its distinctive rationale and rich imaginative resources on the same basis as the institutional aspects of Islam where the message took form, albeit with the same rational basis, despite its different preoccupations and agenda. The most one can do is to study Sufism as an historical and social phenomenon of past, present and possibly future significance, influencing the course of political, economic and social affairs, as well as shaping intellectual life. This approach doubtless neglects the basic spiritual dimension of Sufism, which strives to explore the depths of the prophetic message or rather messages, transcending the limits of time and space, relying on "taste" rather than reason, freed from the pressure and heavy constraints of those who proclaim themselves "guardians of the sanctuary".

The origins of Sufism can be located within an ascetic aspiration, common to a minority in all religions, for freedom, partial or complete, from the burdens of this world, the constraints of money and labour, in order to prepare for death and the annihilation of the body.[68] After the departure of the Prophet this small group within the Muslim community drew spiritual sustenance from meditation on the verses of the Qur'an which emphasise the transient nature of the world and the proximity of the world to come. They cite as a warning the fate of those who store up treasures of gold and silver and do not spend it according to God's designs, while describing the pleasures awaiting the righteous and the punishment in store for the unbelievers. This tendency, in fact, existed among the generation of the Companions and the names of the most illustrious are immortalised in the numerous hagiographical works that are dedicated to them. Asceticism, albeit as a marginal phenomenon, also existed in subsequent generations, influencing small groups known for their piety and moral refinement. They often tended to congregate in frontier posts and fortified monasteries where they combined prayer with participation in holy war.

It is certain that this variety of asceticism has been a permanent feature of Islam, nourishing the Muslim conscience and its reflection on the teachings of the Qur'an and the imitation of the Prophet. It was not calculated to satisfy those who imagined that by reining in the powers of thought and the imagination they could fit different temperaments and dispositions into the same pre-prepared mould and weave all the variegated threads of reality into a single seamless garment. Asceticism would not have evolved into mysticism, that is to say, a lifestyle with common bases and characteristics, were it not for two principal factors which converged to produce renewed dynamism.

First, the refined civilisation of the Abbasid period, marked by elegance and delicacy in numerous aspects of life alongside immorality and debauchery in certain circles constituted a strange and unfamiliar way of life for those used to a frugal existence.[69] Some individuals were offended by these developments and the values that accompanied them. For a variety of reasons they were unable to adapt to these changes. Seen in this light Sufism is a reaction against a particular turn of events rather than a development of a previously existing tendency. Like any reaction, it is prone to move too far in the contrary direction, denouncing the broad sweep of life in this world as error, things forbidden and permitted alike, with the exception of marriage. This is noteworthy, as celibacy was not part of the traditions inherited from the Prophet and, while this practice was characteristic of Christian monasticism, Sufism did not want to be assimilated to Christian monks. There was, it seems, no greater a tendency among Sufis to refrain from marriage than there was the case in other social categories.

The dominant role of 'ulamā' in defining the external practice of faith was another element which contributed ultimately to the development of Sufism. Such external practices are the guarantee of group cohesion, and may be suffi-cient for the general run of believers with their quotidian preoccupations. It is natural that they may not provide adequate spiritual sustenance for smaller groups of believers who desire to go beyond compliance with external liturgical observances and social duties. Such groups give importance to the demands of the conscience in its quest for inner serenity and harmony between what is and that to which the soul aspires. The Sufis were restless and turbulent in character, avid to discover the secrets of existence and explore its mysteries. Many of them preferred to isolate themselves and retreat from the cares of life. They practised meditative introspection and spiritual exercises which they thought would lead them to free themselves from the bonds of the flesh and reach the highest degrees of intimacy with God.

This existential quest proceeded, unbridled, in all directions. It is unsurprising that it led to theories and positions which were to a greater or lesser extent distant from the forms and content of belief fixed by the 'ulamā' and approved by the community, for example, a certain detachment from rites and observations, the affirmation that the divine principle resided in the innermost part of the believ-er's soul, which was capable of union with God. This led to violent opposition from the *fuqahā'*, who solicited assistance from the holders of political power in order to counter Sufi tendencies. The trial and crucifixion of al-Hallāj in the year 309/922 marked the end of an era in the history of Sufism during which it had been independent from the ascetic movements and existed as an intel-lectual current on the fringes of the *fiqh* schools and political factions. After the death of al-Hallāj the number of those rallying to the Sufi cause increased and its leaders sought to obtain the neutrality of the *fuqahā'* and the religious estab-lishment in general, recognising the latter's right to look after what the Sufis considered the external husk of religion as distinct from the kernel of veneration and prayer. This tactical concession did not prevent the infiltration of gnostic ideas and the influence of illuminist philosophy. This incited the *Ahl al-Sunna* to maintain their attitude of circumspection and defend the purity of the faith in conformity with the ideals of the first generations of believers. This could entail violent confrontations with the Sufis, as happened in the case of Shihāb al-Din al-Suhrawardi, assassinated in the year 587/1191 of the Hijra.

Sufism nevertheless continued, despite this opposition, to occupy an important place in the life of Muslims. It gained many new adepts from different social classes, who followed the Sufi way and rose up the degrees of the spiritual hierarchy. The roles played by al-Ghazāli, who introduced Sufism into the Sunni world despite fierce debate, and eminent figures such as the *sheikh al-akbar*, Ibn al 'Arabi (who died in the year 632/1234), were especially important. Sufism would not have expanded as it did across the Muslim world were it not for its pyramidal structure which placed aspirants and those following the spiritual path under the authority of their masters, in a spirit of self-renunciation and obedience to their masters' orders. The gathering of Sufi adepts in *zāwiyas* and *khānaqāh* (convent-style structures) in order to carry out regular rituals and collective spiritual exercises also contributed to its spread. This was also one of the reasons for the cohesion of the broad Sufi community and the solidarity characterising their way of life.

Sufism ceased to evolve from the sixth/thirteenth century onwards, in the same way as any organisation lacking democratic rules for its functioning. It became a confraternity, with its positive and negative aspects. Among the former one may mention the spiritual framework it provided for ordinary people in a period of political fragmentation and the concomitant limiting of the 'ulamā' activity to urban centres. Many Sufi leaders played an effective role in defending the weak and oppressed and in resisting foreign invasion right up until modern times; the cases of this include the Emir 'Abd el-Qādir's resistance to French colonisation in Algeria and Sanusi resistance to the Italians in Libya.[70] The negative aspects of the confraternities were also numerous, transmitting to Sufism a predisposition to offer stubborn resistance to the nineteenth-century reformist movements. Sufism was considered responsible for the spirit of fatalism, and belief in spectacular wonders and miracles were attributed to Sufi "saints". This was due to the contagion of popular piety and the observance of pagan rituals unconnected with Islam. Exploitation and corruption also flourished among Sufi sheikhs. Summing up the main characteristics of Sufism, one may conclude that it was a phenomenon with two main facets. It sustained its adepts in many cases by a rich spiritual life, leading them to high degrees of rapture to which Sufi literature bears witness in works still admired today. These inspire Muslims and non-Muslims alike. At the same time Sufism tended toward self-absorption and a flight from reality, abandoning any attempt to improve it by appropriate means.

In conclusion, Sufism was an ambiguous phenomenon, a fruit of its own particular reading of the message of Islam and of human history. In its later phases it was one of the factors contributing to decadence and decline.

Notes

Introduction

1. See Abdou Filai Ansari, *Réformer l'Islam* (Paris, 2003), pp. 238–241.
2. *Contemporary Islamic Questions* 24/25, summer and autumn 2003, p. 68.
3. Sūra 18:9–26.
4. See Charfi's article in the review قضايا إسلاميّة معاصرة (*Contemporary Muslim Affairs*), 24/25, 2003, pp. 72–3.
5. Ibn al-Kalbi, *The Book of Idols*, trans. Nabih Amin Faris (Princeton, NJ, 1952), pp. 16–17.
6. Hamdi Al Muhammad, الرّائد والدّليل لمعرفة مشارق الوحي ومهابط التنزيل (*The Directory and Guide to the World and the Cradle of Revelation*) (Egypt, 1328/1910).
7. Charfi, p. 76.

History and Theory

1. See Raffaele Pettazzoni (1883–1938) *Religione e Società* (Bologna, 1966), p. 220, and the introduction by M. Meslin, p. 15. Al-Karmānī affirms that God cannot be perceived by the senses as He is not part of the material universe. He is not intelligible, nor does language have the capacity to describe him. Humans are, by their nature, unable to know him and the essence of God is itself beyond the capacity of human perception. See راحة العقل, (*Repose of the Intellect*) (Cairo, 1373/1953), as well as the posthumously published and unjustly little known *Dieu*, a three-volume work by the nineteenth-century French author, Victor Hugo.
2. See Peter Berger, *The Social Reality of Religion* (London, 1973), Part I, pp. 13–107, and Berger's earlier work, *The Sacred Canopy: Elements of a Sociological Theory of Religion* (London, 1967).
3. On the subject of ancient religions one can usefully consult the work of the Romanian scholar Mircea Eliade. See, for example, *The Sacred and the Profane: the Nature of Religion* and *History of Religious Ideas*, 3 vols (Chicago, 1979, 1982, 1985).

4. *Pace* Gilbert Durand, for whom eating the fruit of the tree means death, not knowledge. See Gilbert Durand, *Les structures anthropologiques de l'imaginaire* (Paris, 1973), p. 125.

5. See in particular Ahmad Shahlan, مفهوم الأمية في القرآن ('The meaning of al-*Ummiya* in the Qur'an), مجلة كلية الأدب و العلوم الإنسانية جامعة محمد الخامس (*Arts and Human Sciences Faculty Review*), Muhammad V University, No. 1, 1397/1977, pp. 103–25. This researcher concludes that "al-'Ummiyyīn' are people without scripture or religion, who have remained at the level of their primeval instincts. They have no knowledge of an authentic revelation".

6. See the first chapter of the present author's doctoral thesis, "Arab thought's reply to Christians", الفكر الإسلامي في الرد- على النصارى ('Tunis/Algiers, 1986).

7. An example of this kind of approach is Jacqueline Chabbi's *Le seigneur des tribus. L'islam de Mahomet* (Paris, 1997). This work is evidently based on wide and detailed research and endeavours to apply a philological approach. One has the impression, however, that the author does not, as one might put it, see the wood for the trees, because of the lack of a broad historical view situating Islam within monotheism.

8. Works such as A. Lods, *Israel des origines au viiie siècle avant notre ère* (Paris, 1930), *Les prophètes d'Israel et les débuts du judaïsme* (Paris, 1935), *La religion d'Israel* (Paris, 1939) and Max Weber, *Antike Judentum* (translated into English under the title of *Ancient Judaism*) form the mainstay of the bibliography on this subject.

9. See Christian Defebvre (ed.), *Histoire des religions en Europe: judaïsme, christianisme, et islam* (Paris, 1999).

10. See Victor Sahab, ايلاف قرايش ('*The unification of Quraysh*) (Beirut, 1992).

11. Jean Duvignaud, *Change at Shebika: Report from a North African Village*, trans. Frances Frenaye (Austin, TX, 1977), p. 83: "The observance of tradition is actually a factor in the dissolution of structures."

The Preaching of Muhammad

1. Mircea Eliade, *Briser le toit de la maison* (Paris, 1986), p. 316: "Every historical character is transformed by popular memory into a mythical hero, while his personal history acquires exemplary status."

2. Contemporary and traditional biographies rely on sources such as Ibn Sa'd (طبقات, "*categories*") and Ibn Hishām (سيرة, "*biography*"), although these sources contain only fragmentary anecdotes which do not meet the requirements of the historian. See محمّد قبل البعثة Abdallah Jennouf, (*Muhammad before his Prophetic Mission*) (Faculty of Arts and Humanities, Manouba, 1999).

3. See Muhammad Hamidullah, "Les voyages du Prophète avant l'islam", *Bulletin d'études orientales*, XXIX (1977), pp. 221–30.

4. Georges Dumézil, *Mythes et dieux des Indo-Européens* (Paris, 1992), p. 239.

5. Ibn al-Kalbi, كتاب الأصنام (*The Book of Idols*) (Cairo, 1384/1965), p. 19. Ibn al-Kalbi adds that Quraysh "went in procession around the Kaaba crying out: 'By Lāt and al-'Uzza and by Manāh, the third: these are the sublime goddesses whose intercession is to be hoped for.'" This invocation comprises what are known as "the Satanic verses". A tradition mentioned by Ibn Ishāq in the *Sīra* confirms that Muhammad took part, as "a young

man" in sacrifices offered to idols. According to this tradition, "Zayd ibn Amr ibn Nufayl denounced the idols and those who worship them and sacrifice to them. 'They are worthless', he said, 'and do no harm nor good". Muhammad went on: 'I never addressed any request after that to any of the idols, nor did I sacrifice to them until God honoured me with his message.' 'This Zayd', he said, 'was the first to denounce the idols in my presence and forbid me to have dealings with them.' He refused to eat the meat that Muhammad presented to him 'coming from our sacrifices to the idols'." كتاب الأصنام (*The Book of Idols*) (Rabat, 1396/1976), p. 98.

6. The following verses were subsequently revealed to Muhammad: "Surely thou art upon a high morality" (Sūra 68:4). "Hadst thou been harsh and hard of heart, they would have scattered from about thee." (Sūra 3:159).

7. It is not certain, though, that she was forty years old, as the traditions contained in the *Sira* ("biography") recount. When she married Muhammad, who was then around twenty-five years old, perhaps she was no more than thirty years old or a little older. Salwa Bel Haj Sālih al-Ayeb examines the figure of Khadīja in her book, دثريني يا خديجة (*daththirīnī Khadīja*) (Beirut, 1999).

8. Muhammad Abduh, رسالة التوحيد (*The Letter on the Unity of God*) (Cairo, 1343/1925), p. 108. Mustapha Abd-al-Rāziq says in this connection: "One can note that dominant opinion among Muslims about revelation inclines towards the position of the theologians during periods of intellectual stagnation while in periods of renewal it aligns itself more with the viewpoints of the philosophers." Commenting on the point of view of Muhammad Abduh he says: "This is the point of view of the philosophers even if the notes in the margins expound the opinions of the theologians," الدين والوحي و الإسلام (*Religion, Revelation Islam*) (Cairo, 1364/1945), p. 80.

9. Khadīja said to him: "Rejoice, cousin and stand firm! By He who holds Khadīja's life in His hand, I hope truly that you will be the prophet of this people." Waraqa, for his part, said: "The great Nâmûs who visited Moses has come to him. Verily, he will be the prophet of this people." Ibn Hisham, السيرة النبوية (*Biography of the Prophet*) (Zarqa, Jordan, 1409/1988), I, pp. 301–2. A similar tradition can be found, attributed to Aicha, in the صحيح *Sahih* of al-Bukhāri in the chapter entitled "On the interpretation of the Qur'an", Sūra 96).

10. "He [Gabriel] it was that brought it down upon your heart by the leave of God, confirming what was before it, and for a guidance and good tidings to the unbelievers." (Sūra 2:97).

11. Sūra 26:192–5: "Truly it is the revelation of the Lord of all Being, brought down by the Faithful Spirit upon thy heart, that thou mayest be one of the warners, in a clear, Arabic tongue." Sūra 2:97: "Say: 'Whosoever is an enemy of Gabriel – he it was that brought it down upon thy heart by the leave of God ...'" It is curious that conservatives should have protested when Fazlur Rahman declared, basing his remarks on these two verses, that "Orthodoxy ... lacked the intellectual capacity to say both that the Quran is entirely the Word of God and, in an ordinary sense, also entirely the word of Muhammad." See Fazlur Rahman, *Islam* (Chicago, 1386/1966), p. 31. We have noted, in this regard, the opinion of Hichām Djait according to which the "prophet receives the revelation merely in a passive manner", الوحي والقرآن و النبوّ (*Inspiration, the Qur'an, Prophethood*) (Beirut, 1999), p. 70.

This observation is inconsistent with the overall analysis of prophecy and inspiration presented by the author in the rest of his text.

12. Sūra 19:97: "Now We have made it easy by thy tongue that thou mayest bear good tidings thereby to the godfearing, and warn a people stubborn."

13. See al Suyūti, الإتقان *al-Itqān*, ch. 10, "Concerning what was revealed of the Qur'an to some of the Companions". See too al-Zamakhshari, الكشّاف (*al-Kashshāf*) (Beirut, undated), pp. 299 and 310. See, too, the chapter entitled "Reading religious heritage" in our publication لبنات (*Building Bricks*) (Tunis, 1994), pp. 113–29.

14. Al-Suyūti adds that "the person who affirms this retains the evident meaning of the Almighty's message: 'The spirit of faithfulness descended on your heart'" (Sūra 26:193). See الإتقان (*al-Itqān*), ch. 16, "How revelation happened". This shows that traditional scholars could be more flexible than many of their contemporaries.

15. This belief is encountered throughout collections of hadith (accounts of what the Prophet did or what he tacitly approved), in works of theology and Qur'anic studies. See Mustapha Abd al-Rāziq, الدين والوحي و الإسلام (*Religion, Revelation Islam*) as well as Fazlur Rahman's *Prophecy in Islam: Philosophy and Orthodoxy* (London, 1958), where he studies prophecy in the work of Ibn Sīna in particular, along with al-Farābi, Ibn Hazm, al-Ghazāli, al-Shahrastani, Ibn Taymiyya and Ibn Khaldoun. See, too, Ali Mabrūk, النبوّة (*Prophecy*) (Cairo, 1993), in which the author, relying on modern research, presents the phenomenon of prophecy in the pre-Islamic period. Then he moves on to Muslim theological texts, without examining the nature of Muhammad's prophecy except in one somewhat convoluted and timorous note on p. 100.

16. Abu Ridha (ed.), رسائل الكندي الفلسفيّة (*The Philosophical Letters of al-Kindi*) (Cairo, 1370/1950), p. 373. Al-Farābi, أراء أهل المدينة الفضيلة (*Ideas of the Inhabitants of the Virtuous City*) (Beirut, 1379/1959), p. 94.

17. Max Weber (1864–1920), German sociologist.

18. See Lucien Febvre, *Le problème de l'incroyance au xvie siècle. La religion de Rabelais* (Paris, 1968).

19. See Nasr Hamid Abu Zayd, مفهوم النص (*The Meaning of Text*) (Beirut/Casablanca, 1996), p. 24: "The Qur'an describes itself as being a message. The message supposes a link between the person sending the message and the person receiving it, through a code or a linguistic system. In the case of the Qur'an, the Sender of the message could not be the object of scientific study. It is therefore natural that the text be studied through the prism of culture and historical circumstances."

20. Ibn Hishām, السيرة (*al-Sīra*), vol. 2, pp. 92–4, 176–8, 288–93. It is noteworthy that the latter tradition mentions that when the Prophet dispatched the leader of the exhibition, he gave him a document requesting him not to read it until two days" march were completed. This suggests that the Prophet could write as the order refers to a secret written message. Another tradition which appears on p. 87 of the same volume suggests that Abu Amama As'as ibn Zurar was the first to gather together the Muslims in Medina for prayer, an initiative subsequently approved by the Prophet.

21. "And We know very well that they say 'Only a mortal is teaching him'. The speech of him at whom they hint is barbarous; and this is speech Arabic, manifest." (Sūra 16:103) See,

too, the numerous verses where the charge of forgery is directed against the Prophet: "They say, 'fairy tales of the ancients that he has written down, so that they are recited to him at the dawn and in the evening'" (Sūra 25:5); "Or do they say, 'He has forged against God a lie?'" (Sūra 42:24), for example.

22. "Say: 'I do not say to you, I posses the treasuries of God; I know not the Unseen. And I say not to you, I am an angel; I only follow what was revealed to me.'" (Sūra 6:50); "Say: 'I have no power to profit for myself or hurt, but as God will. Had I knowledge of the Unseen I would have acquired much good, and evil would not have touched me.'" (Sūra 7:188).

23. For example: "Say: 'It is not for me to alter it of my own accord.'" (Sūra 10:15); "this Qur'an could not have been forged apart from God".

24. "And all that We relate to thee of the tidings of the Messengers is that whereby We strengthen thy heart" (Sūra 11:120).

25. "Or do they say, he has forged it? Say: If I have forged it, you have no power to help me against God. He knows very well what you are pressing upon; He suffices as a witness between me and you; He is the All-forgiving, the All-compassionate" (Sūra 46:8).

26. Sūra 2:53, 87, 89, 92, 97, 159, 136, 213, 251, 253; Sūra 3:48, 184; Sūra 4:163; Sūra 5:48; Sūra 7:144; Sūra 10:47, etc. See Muḥammad Fuād al-Bāqi, معجم المفهرس لألفاظ القرآن (*Dictionary of Terms of the Noble Quran*) (Cairo: numerous editions).

27. When the daughter of Khālid ibn Sinān al-'Absi came to see him, he exclaimed: "She is the daughter of a prophet condemned by his own people." Jāhiz, الحيوأن (*The Book of Animals*) (Beirut, 1969/1377), vol. 4, p. 477.

28. Sūra 2:89, 97; Sūra 5:48; Sūra 6:92; Sūra 10:37, etc.

29. One may note that the evil spirits are presented by the Qur'an as being mere creatures of God. Muslims do not have to worship them or make offerings, contrary to popular belief. Concerning the Flood, the discovery of the Babylonian epic of Gilgamesh texts in 1872 caused consternation among committed Jews and Christians, as these texts contain an account of a flood similar to that contained in Chapters 6 to 8 of the Book of Genesis. With regard to miracles in the Qur'an, the doctoral thesis of Wahīd al-Sa'fi, تفسير ابن كثير نموذجاً العجيب و الغريب في كتب تفسير القرآن (Faculty of Arts and Humanities, Manouba, 1999), can be consulted. This may shed light on Muhammad Abduh's refusal to accept that the Qur'an intended to make reference to historical events, as Muhammad Ahmad Khalfallah attempted to demonstrate in his thesis, الفنّ القصصي في القرآن الكريم (*Narrative Art in the noble Qur'an*) (Cairo, 1376/1957).

30. See J. Lambert, *Le dieu distribué* (Paris, 1996), p. 78 for the following definition of prophecy: "Cette commune ouverture, qui est à la fois une invention unique, mais homologue, par laquelle une fraction du people veut échapper aux injustices consti-tuées du social en les dépassant par une radicalité inouïe de la fidélité. Le prophétisme n'est donc pas seulement le censeur des injustices. Il en est le rejeton critique comme le printemps sur l'arbre de l'élan spirituel."

Distinctive Characteristics of Muhammad's Message

1. Henri Bergson, French philosopher (1859–1941).

2. Nasr Hamid Abu Zaid, مفهوم النصّ,(*The Meaning of Text*), pp. 108–15.

3. See, for example, al-Suyūti, الإتقان (*al-Itqān*) (*Precision and Mastery in the Sciences of the Qur'an*), ch. 18: "Collection and classification of the Qur'an". Professor Muhammad Talbi, in a UNESCO Chair of Comparative Religions lecture given on 15 May 2000 at the Faculty of Arts and Humanities, Manouba, suggested that the Qur'an was not recorded with the primitive means mentioned by the existing traditions. Parchment would have been used, according to the following verses: "By the mountain, and by the Scripture penned on unrolled parchment!" (Sūra 52:1–3). This sūra (*al Tūr*) is Meccan: it cannot, therefore, designate the whole Qur'an, nor does the term "book", as we shall presently see, have a material sense.

4. Ibn abi Daoud, mentions that 'Uthmān, when asked about the *Mashaf*, said: "It contains grammatical faults which the Arabs will correct as they pronounce." See المصاحف (*The Volumes*) (Cairo, 1356/1937), p. 32. He quotes too the question put by Ali to those who rebelled against 'Uthmān: "What do you reproach him with?" They answered: "we reproach him with having destroyed the Book of God" (*Ibid.*, p. 36). Tabari, for his part, notes that the dissidents said: "The Qur'an existed in several versions: you have kept only one." See التاريخ (Cairo, 1390/1970), part IV, p. 347. 'Uthmān's initiative was highly symbolic: this act, rather than his nepotism or any other motive retained by the collective memory, provoked opposition to him.

5. See on this point the *Sahīh* of al-Bukhāri, the book of فضائل القرآن (*Merits of the Qur'an*), chapter entitled, أنزل القرآن على سبعة أحرف (The Qur'an was revealed in seven variant readings) where it is said that the Prophet authorised the readings of 'Umār ibn al-Khattāb and Hishām ibn Hakīm. This authorisation led to the hesitations, and ultimate apostasy of 'Abdallah ibn Said ibn Abī Sarh, one of those who transcribed the revelation. See Ibn al-Athīr, أسد الغابة (*Asad al-Ghāba*) (Cairo, 1390/1970), III/259, and al-Balādhuri, *Futūh al-buldān* (Cairo, 1350/1932), p. 459. Al-Suyūti, in ch. 16 of *al-Itqān*, recounts how 'Abdallah ibn Mas'ūd recited before someone "The tree of Zaqqūm is the food of the criminal." The man said: "the food of the orphan". But 'Abdallah stood by his story. His interlocutor said: "could you say: 'the food of the wastrel?'" 'Abdallah replied "yes". "Then do so", came the reply. On the flexibility that characterises oral religious discourse over written forms, see Jack Goody, *La logique de l'Ecriture* (Paris, 1986), p. 21.

6. See J. Van Ess, "Une lecture à rebours de l'histoire du mu'tazilisme", *Revue d'études islamiques,* vol. LXVI, fasc. 2, 1978, pp. 185–94.

7. See Ze'ev Herzog, "Deconstructing the walls of Jericho", *Haaretz*, 19 October 1999, pp. 1–8. Françoise Smyth-Florentin has illustrated this point in several articles.

8. They naturally refuse, along with inadequately-informed Muslims, the principle of evolution. As François Jacob, a leading contemporary French scientist, puts it:"we are to imagine, therefore, that all the animals on the earth today descend from a single organism which lived 600 hundred million years ago and already possessed this variety of genes." *Le Monde*, 4 January 2000, p. 14.

9. "The unbelievers of the People of the Book and the pagans did not desist from unbelief

until the Clear Sign came to them: an apostle from God reading pages purified, therein true books" Sūra 98:2–3). See too Sūra 80:11–16: "No indeed; it is a Reminder (and who so wills, shall remember it) upon pages high-honoured, uplifted, purified, by the hands of scribes noble, pious."

10. See Wilferd F. Madelung, "The origins of the controversy concerning the creation of the Qur'an", in *Orientalia Hispanica*, vol. I, 1974, pp. 504–25 and Fahmi Jad'ān بحث في المهنة جدلية الديني و السياسي في الإسلام (*The Mihna: Study of the Controversy between Religion and Politics in Islam*) (Amman, 1989).

11. Sūra 18:109. See, too, Emmanuel Levinas' quotation of the words of Rabbi Eliezer in *Difficult Freedom: essays on Judaism* (London, 1990), p. 29: "If all the seas were ink, reeds pens, the heavens parchment and all men writers, they would not suffice to write down the Torah I have learned, and the Torah itself would be diminished only by the amount drawn out of it by the tip of a paintbrush dipped in the sea."

12. Sūra 56:77–80.

13. Mahmoud Muhammad Taha, Sudanese scholar hanged in January 1985 after being found guilty of anti-Islamic activities. الرسالة الثانية من الإسلام (*The Second Message of Islam*) was first published in the Sudan in 1967 and reprinted several times.

14. See the present author's الإسلام و الحداثة (*Islam and Modernity*) (Tunis, 1990) for a detailed commentary on each of these positions.

Legislation

1. Sūra 45:12 "And now we have set you on the right path. Follow it ..."

2. This is the point that Muhammad Talbi made, using the image of the "pointed arrow" (السهم الموجه). See his book, 'عيال الله" (*The families of God*) (Tunis, 1992).

3. The only occasion when details are given is in Sūra 4:101–2. Abū Hanifa nevertheless maintained that Muslims were dispensed from prayer if, in the thick of battle, fear was running high. Prayer could be postponed in this case.

4. Rāzī (*c.* 239/854–*c.* 312/925) nevertheless noted that the Companions disagreed about features of the Prophet's behaviour which one might suppose they had seen on numerous occasions: "Despite their constant preoccupation with religious matters and their zeal in observing its rites, the Companions were unable to carry out exactly gestures which they had seen five times a day: stand up once or twice, reciting aloud, raising the hands." See Rāzī's, المحصول (*al-Mahsūl*) (Beirut, 1412/1992), vol. 1, p. 214. He goes on to say that: "Standing up once or twice is one of the most common actions, although this prescription has not been uninterruptedly handed down from one generation to the next. Actions such as raising the hands or saying bismillah in a loud voice are also matters which are clear and evident although they have not been handed down uninterruptedly across the generations." *Ibid.*, vol. IV, p. 293.

5. A rapid survey of the myriad details contained in the books of *fiqh* across the range of juridical schools reveals the gulf between them and the Qur'an, which insists simply on the need to pray. These details are relevant to a type of society which has disappeared or is in the course of doing so, given its archaic way of life and obsolete or obsolescent means of production.

6. The classic work on this subject, although written from a Christian viewpoint, is that of Friedrich Heiler, translated into English under the title of *Prayer, a Study in the History and Psychology of Religion* (Oxford University Press, 1932).

7. Dr. Mahmoud Sidqi first raised this question in modern times concerning prayer and alms-giving in his article, "الإسلام هو القرآن وحده" ("Islam: the Qur'an alone"), in the review, المنار (*al-Manār*), No. 9, 1324/1906, pp. 515–25.

8. Charfi, لبنات (*Building Bricks*), pp. 165–83.

9. Muhammad Hamidullah, "Le musulman dans le milieu occidental", in *Normes et valeurs dans l'islam contemporain* (Paris, 1966), pp. 200–5. Muslims living in these regions, northern Europe and America, are not a scattered handful of individuals but number in their millions. They are mainly immigrants or their descendants, although they include local converts to Islam. They far outnumber the Muslim communities existing at the time of the Prophet.

10. Consultation of the commentaries concerned with the prescriptive verses demonstrates this. See, for example, أحكام القرآن (*Prescriptive Verses of the Qur'an*) by al-Jassās, al-Kiyā' al-Harāsi, and Ibn al-Arabi, and even الجامع لأحكام القرآن (*Collection of Prescriptive Verses in the Qur'an*) by al-Qurtubi.

11. See in particular Amel Grami م قضية الردّة في الفكر الإسلا (*Apostasy in Islamic Thought*) (Faculty of Arts and Humanities, Manouba, 1993). The central thesis of Muhammad Charfi's book, *Islam et liberté* (Paris, 1998) is the incompatibility of freedom and *fiqh* with regard to this question and many others.

12. One such example of this deviation from the essential truth of Islam, representative of a widespread and multiform tendency, was to be found in the Tunisian daily newspaper, الصباح (*al-Sabāh*), on Sunday, 20 February 1994, p. 6: "One of the most important rules for inculcating good manners is to obey the Word of God 'If you have disobeyed, conceal yourself from view'." This false idea, which encourages hypocrisy, went unchallenged by the editor of the paper and its readers.

13. "And the thief, male and female, cut off the hands of both as a recompense for what they have earned, and a punishment exemplary from God; God is all-mighty, all-wise." (Sūra 5:38).

14. Abdelmadjid Charfi تحديث الفكر الإسلامي, (*Modernising Islamic Thought*) (Casablanca, 1998), pp. 49–51. See also Nā'ila Sallīnī تاريخية التفسير القرآني و العلاقات الاجتماعية ("The Historicity of Quranic Commentary and Social Relations") (doctoral thesis, Faculty of Arts and Humanities, Manouba, 1998), pp. 166–93.

15. Muhammad Iqbal, *The Reconstruction of Religious Thought in Islam* (Oxford University Press, 1950), p. 157 and 163.

16. On interest and usury see Abdullah Saeed, *Islamic Banking and Interest. A Study of the Prohibition of Riba and its Contemporary Interpretation* (Leiden, 1996). This excellent and well-documented account confirms the documentation assembled by the present author in الإسلام و الحداثة (*Islam and Modernity*) concerning the fraudulent methods employed by banks who boast they are applying the Sharī'a while merely changing the names of the operations they carry out. It was also noted in the above work that the Sheikh of al-Azhar

went so far as to denounce the so-called Islamic banks in 1998, giving preference to conventional institutions.

17. This separation does not apply in all circumstances, even if democratic systems generally prevent the state from manipulating religion. Thus, former US President, George Bush Sr., declared in a widely-diffused speech to troops departing for the Gulf in August 1990 that "the world's eyes are fixed upon you and the hopes and prayers of all those who love freedom go with you". The American branch of the Catholic Pax Christi (Peace of Christ) movement replied that for a war to be just it needs to be the last resort. In Pax Christi's view, this was not the case in the Gulf War. War should not be waged on innocents in order to preserve energy interests and Western lifestyles.

18. Tabari's commentary on the Sūra al-Tawba sheds ample light on the real stakes of this expedition, although his text also contains elements related to events which happened after the time of Muhammad.

19. See the chapter "Islam and Violence" in Charfi, لبنات (*Building Bricks*), pp. 183–201. We have not seen fit to modify the point of view expressed in that chapter, although it did not take into account the prevailing justification for the conquests under the caliphs 'Umar and Othmān, namely that they were a continuation of the jihād initiated by the Prophet.

20. In this context the Qur'an (Sūra 38:35) mentions that Solomon was the only prophet to rule a kingdom "such as may not befall any after me".

21. This expression is also applied to Abraham, with regard to monotheism: "you have had a good example in Abraham and in those with him, when they said to their people, 'We are quit of you and that you serve, apart from God'" (Sūra 60:4). See also verse 6 of the same Sūra.

22. Such expressions appear throughout the Qur'an in the Meccan and Medinan Sūras. They express a basic principle of the Prophet's message. In the light of this an appreciation is made of the correct conduct to follow in particular circumstances.

23. "But no, by thy Lord! They will not believe till they make thee the judge regarding the disagreement between them, then they shall find in themselves no impediment touching thy verdict, but shall surrender in full submission." (Sūra 4:65). The Prophet was nevertheless conscious of the limits of his human power and never made any claims to perfection, neither when he took the initiative in giving an opinion as in the celebrated incident of the pollination of palm trees, nor when he intervened in disputes. See al-Bukhāri, (*al-Sahīh*), كتاب الأحكام باب من قضى له بحقّ أخيه فلا يأخذها ("The book of prescriptions: the chapter relating to the person in whose favour a judgment is made at the expense of his brother: let him not take what is due to his brother").

24. The opinion of Ali is based on an analogy which does not hold good in all cases: "The drinker gets drunk, when drunk he becomes irrational, then he pronounces words of slander, and the punishment for the slanderer is eighty lashes." On another occasion he said "I would not inflict a mortal punishment on anyone. I can see only the case of the drinker. If he died I would pay the blood price. The Prophet had not decreed that." Rāzi, المحصول (*al-Mahsūl*), IV, p. 190.

25. Al-Khatīb al-Baghdādi (393/1002–464/1071), commenting on this episode, notes that

"this tradition contains two teachings, one which is general, namely that the person who has had sexual relations with his wife during the Ramadan fast must make reparation. The second is specific to this instance, namely the authorization given by the Prophet for the man to appropriate the donation. Only the Prophet can give this kind of authorization." See الفقيه و المتفقه (*al-faqīh wa-l-mutafaqqih*) ("The Legal Specialist and the Scholar Devoted to *fiqh*"), (2nd edn, Beirut, 1400/1980), vol. I, pp. 110–11.

26. Tunisia is considered to have gone further than other Arab countries in promoting women's rights. The Code de statut personnel promulgated in 1957, prohibited polygamy, gave courts sole authority to pronounce divorce and enabled unmarried women to choose their husbands and inherit property in the absence of male relations. This audacious and progressive legislation opened the way to future developments. It challenged customs which deprive women of their most elementary rights, such as that of education, insistence on the segregation of the sexes and forbidding women from driving.

27. "The fornicatress and the fornicator – scourge each of them a hundred stripes, and in the matter of God's religion let no tenderness for them seize you" (Sūra 24:2).

28. "And those who cast it up on women in wedlock, and then bring not four witnesses, scourge them with eighty stripes, and do not accept any testimony of theirs ever; those – they are the ungodly" (Sūra 24:4).

29. "But when they (female slaves) are in wedlock, if they commit indecency, they shall be liable to half the punishment of freedwomen" (Sūra 4:25).

30. See Shahlān Hā'iri, المتعة الزواج المؤقّت عند الشيعة (*Al-Mut'a: Temporary Marriage among the Shia*), (7th edn, Beirut, 1996). This was originally a doctoral thesis presented in the United States under the title of "Law of Desire: Temporary Marriage in Iran". Also 'Abdallah Kamāl, الدعارة الحلال (*Legal Prostitution*) (Beirut, 1997). The author studies the زواج المتعة, "temporary marriage" (literal translation: "marriage of pleasure") in Iran, traditional marriage in Egypt, and the زواج المسيار "marriage of facility" in the Arabian peninsula.

31. An example of this was the refusal of the Jordanian parliament in late 1999 to modify the law authorising the killing of an adulteress (and not the adulterer) by a member of her family. Many women, married and single are victims of this practice, often because of suspicion, rumours, or calumny. There is nothing Islamic or Qur'anic about such behaviour.

32. "Sexual relations, except where children are concerned, are a strictly private matter concerning neither the state nor one's neighbour. Certain sexual practices which do not lead to procreation are punishable by the law: this is mere superstition. The importance attached to adultery is totally irrational. Many other kinds of reprehensible behaviour do more damage to the happiness of a couple than a passing infidelity." B. Bussel, *Pourquoi je ne suis pas chrétien* (Paris, 1972), p. 77.

The Seal of Prophecy

1. Muhammad Iqbal, *The Reconstruction of Religious Thought in Islam* (London, 1934), p. 120.

2. One may note that the Qur'an makes no mention of "rites of passage" such as circumcision and excision which are mentioned in the *hadīth* collection. Historical research could show whether such customs existed at the period during which the *hadīth* were

collected or at the time of revelation.

3. Iqbal, *The Reconstruction of Religious Thought in Islam*, p. 120.

4. "Muhammad is not the father of any one of your men, but the Messenger of God and the Seal of the prophets. God has knowledge of everything" (Sūra 33:40). We will not discuss here the popular understanding of the term "seal". The need to give a material translation for abstract terms such as "seal" is the reason for the way in which the *Sīra* texts (biographical and hagiographic texts) speak of a visible seal between the shoulders of the Prophet, one of the signs of prophecy. See, for example, Ibn 'Ishāq, *Sīra* (Ribat, 1976), p. 69.

5. The *Sīra* texts, particularly the later ones, abound with examples of these miracles considered by popular imagination as indispensable attributes of prophetic perfection. See, for example, al-Qādi Iyādh's الشفاءفي التعريف بحقوق المصطفى (*Healing in the Recognition of the Chosen One*). This is unsurprising given that similar miracles, called *karamāt*, were attributed to saints and holy men, although they were very similar to those attributed to the Prophet.

6. The Baha'is hold the same belief, maintaining that although the prophetic line has been concluded, prophets may still appear after Muhammad: they hold that the founder of their religion, Bahā'u'lláh, lived in the nineteenth century. See Moncef b. Abdeljelil, الفرقة الهامشية في الإسلام (*Marginal Sects in Islam*) (Tunis, 1999).

7. This explains why the conduct of the Ghuzz tribesmen amazed the tenth-century geographer and traveller, Ibn Fadhlān: "When they agree about something and decide to act, the lowest and most miserable of them come and break the agreement that has been reached. Each of them, not only those with the power to loose and bind as in the Muslim countries, can oppose decisions." Ibn Fadhlān, *Voyage chez les Bulgares de la Volga*, trans. M. Canard (Paris, 1988), p. 38.

8. "And those who answer their Lord and perform the prayer, their affair being counsel between them, and they expend of that which we have provided them" (Sūra 42:38). "So pardon them, and pray forgiveness for them, and take counsel with them in the affair, and when thou art resolved put thy trust in God" (Sūra 3:159).

9. Sūra 33:45; Sūra 33:21.

10. The way in which the freedom at the heart of the message of Islam is obscured by the confusion between politics and religion did not escape the attention of the German theologian, Eugen Drewermann: "Although Islam can rightly be termed a religion of liberty, the way in which politics and religion are closely associated in a way that recalls the Middle Ages appears today as something anti-libertarian." Eugen Drewermann, *Fonctionnaires de Dieu* (Paris, 1993), p. 732.

11. The case of the Italian astronomer, Galileo (1564–1642) is one example of this, as well as the Church's recognition of the principle of freedom of conscience which it had vigorously resisted. The Church is now cautiously expressing its regret about its silence during the Nazi persecution of the Jews. The Church has not yet addressed the question of its support for slavery and colonialism in the past, whether in Latin America or Africa.

12. Concerning the 'ulamā' and the religious establishment in the Sunni system, see: المؤسسة الدينية في الإسلام ("The Religious Institution in Islam"), in لبنات (*Building Bricks*), pp. 69–84.

13. See Jürgen Habermas, *The Structural Transformation of the Public Sphere* (Oxford, 1999). The public sphere is a social site where collective rationality, as distinct from individual and group interests, can express itself.

Part Two Introduction

1. These Caliphs (the *Rāshidūn*) were Abū Bakr (10/632–12/634), 'Umar (12/634–24/644) and 'Uthmān (24/644–35/656).
2. This is to be differentiated from research based on preconceived ideas which strip Islam of its specificity and apply categories derived from Judaism and Christianity. This leads to claims that the Qur'an took on its final form only in the third/ninth century. See Patricia Crone and Michael Cook's *Hagarism: the Making of the Islamic World* (Cambridge University Press, 1977), and John Wansbrough's *Quranic Studies: Sources and Methods of Scriptural Interpretation* (Oxford University Press, 1977).
3. The *Sahāba* (Companions) are those who personally knew the Prophet. The *Tābiūn* are those who were not contemporaries of the Prophet but knew one of the *Sahāba*.
4. See Max Weber, *L'éthique protestante et l'esprit du capitalisme* (Paris, 1985), p. 102 (*The Protestant Ethic and the Spirit of Capitalism* (London, 2001)) and Ernst Troeltsch, *Protestantisme et modernité* (1991).
5. See Khalīl Abd el Karām, شدو الربابة باحوال مجتمع الصحابة (*The Music of the Companions*), 3 vols (Cairo, 1997). The author has collected numerous traditions from biographies of the Prophet, the *Tabaqāt* and historical works, differentiating between historical reality and the idealised version of events concerning the Companions in the collective imagination of Muslim communities.

The Prophet's Successors

1. See Ibn Hishām, *al-Sīra*, vol. II, p. 167–72. This document, also known as the "Constitution", has been the object of much research in order to demonstrate its authenticity or lack thereof.
2. A *saqīfa* is a covered communal area suitable for meetings. The term is used by historians to refer to the negotiations that took place in 11/632 before the nomination of Abū Bakr as head of the incipient community.
3. *Ansār*: inhabitants of Medina who gave their support to Muhammad. *Muhājirūn*: Meccan Muslims who emigrated to Medina with Muhammad or before the conquest of Mecca in 8/630.
4. See A. Guillaume, *The Life of Muhammad: a Translation of Ibn Ishaq's Sīrat Rasul Allāh* (Karachi, 1978), p. 685.
5. See the *Sahih* of al-Bukhāri, book of *hudūd* ("legal punishments"), "Stoning of a married women pregnant as a result of adultery".
6. This is the same point made by the theoreticians of the Caliphate when they quote the pre-Islamic poet from the sixth-century CE al-Afwah al Awdī: "Chaos harms the people that has no leader."
7. In the words of Jāhiz: "The common people do not know the meaning of the term imamate and how to understand the term of caliphate. They cannot distinguish between

Notes

the benefits that the caliphate brings and the resulting harm if the caliphate is vacant. They are unaware of its origins and of how one attains the caliphate. The common mass are carried away by the wind of rumour and novelty and take more pleasure in listening to prattlers and windbags than to those who speak the truth." Jāhiz, رسائل الجاحظ (*Letters of Jāhiz*) (Cairo, 1399/1979), vol. IV, p. 37. Muhammad Abduh echoes this point of view when he says: "The people on whom one can rely to develop the nation, to reflect and bring enlightenment, are those who make up the majority of the middle and upper-ranking members of society, not the rabble and the common herd. If the middle and upper classes reflect wisely, their thoughts are moving towards perfection. If the common people are ignorant and superstitious, they do not prevent progress or stand in the way of civilisation so long as the upper classes remain lucid and thoughtful." Muhammad Abduh, الأعمال الكاملة (*Complete Works*), vol. II, part 2, p. 160.

8. See, in the Old Testament, the Book of Leviticus 15:19–33. Gilbert Durand demonstrated that the Sabbath was sacred for the duration of what was held to be the menstrual period of the lunar goddess Ishtar, once a month, before it was fixed at once a week. According to Durand, the word "sabbath" comes from a root meaning "the dread day of Ishtar". See Durand, *Les structures anthropologiques*, p. 119.

9. Iblīs: the Devil, possibly a contraction of the Greek διάβολος. According to the Qur'an: (Sūra 15:30–3) Iblīs refused to prostrate himself before Adam: "Then the angels bowed themselves all together save Iblīs: he refused to be among those bowing." He tempted Adam and Eve: "And We said, 'Adam, dwell thou, and thy wife, in the Garden and eat thereof easefully where you desire; but draw not nigh this tree, lest you be evildoers.' The Satan caused them to slip therefrom and brought them out of that they were in" (Sūra 2:34–6). At the end of time Iblīs shall be punished: "And Paradise shall be brought forward for the godfearing and Hell advanced for the perverse ... Then they shall be pitched into it, they and the perverse, and the hosts of Iblīs all together" (Sūra 26:90, 94).

10. اسرائليات (*Isra'iliyyāt*): a corpus composed of stories concerning the prophets (قصص الأنبياء (*qisas al anbiyā*)), stories of the ancient Israelites and folklore of Jewish origin.

11. *Ahl al-Kitāb*: Qur'anic term (also employed by Muslim scholars) to designate the Jews and Christians, to whom scriptures had been revealed: Torah (*tawrāh*), Psalter, (*zabūr*), and Gospels (*injīl*).

12. The two verses on which this arbitrary interpretation is based are: "O Prophet, say to thy wives and daughters and the believing women, that they draw their veils close to them; so it is likelier that they will be known, and not hurt. God is All-forgiving, All-compassionate" (Sūra 33:59) and "Let them cast their veils over their bosoms ..." (Sūra 24:31). The first verse merely requests that women should draw their robes close to them so that they may be recognised and avoid being harmed when they go out after dark to answer the call of nature, there being no toilets in the houses of Medina. The second verse forbids a woman to show off her charms by covering her chest so that her breasts will be hidden and not visible over the top of her dress. This is far removed from the prescriptions of the *fuqahā'* who consider the female body as something shameful which should be hidden.

13. Abū Bakr (10/632–12/634), 'Umar (12/634–24/644), and 'Uthmān (24/644–35/656).

14. Plural of *maulan*: client, vassal or dependant.

169

15. A movement which in the later 'Ummayad period refused to recognise the privileged position of the Arabs.

16. Empire was the traditional form of the state in the majority of civilisations. Its most significant characteristics are its shifting frontiers, expanding at periods of strength and declining at times of weakness. Different languages, cultures and even religions coexisted, and its subjects were not subject to one single legal system applied to all those living within stable geographical frontiers, as is the case since the foundation of nation states in the modern era. One of the most important factors in the present-day crisis in Muslim thought is that it has not assimilated or interiorised this profound change affecting the shape of states, kingdoms and emirates. It functions with pre-imperial schemas now devoid of their foundations, continuing to adhere to *fiqh*, for example, although this by its nature is law concerning a particular community which may not live in a state which applies its laws to all its citizens whatever their religion, even if these laws may be influenced by a particular religious heritage. The structures of the modern state, its capacity to enforce compliance and intervene in a wide range of areas go far beyond that of traditional state structures.

17. See Balādhurī, فتوح البلدان (*Book of the Conquests of Lands*), pp. 439–40, for the following tradition: "Abū Hurayra recounts that on his return from Bahrain he went to see 'Umar. He said: 'I met him at the moment of the night prayer, I greeted him, and he asked me for news of our people.' Then he asked me: 'What did you bring?' I said: 'I brought five hundred thousand.' He said 'Do you know what you are saying?' I said: 'One hundred thousand and one hundred thousand and I counted until five hundred thousand.' He said: 'You are sleepy, go back home and rest, come back and see me tomorrow morning.' 'Abū Hurayra added: 'I went back to see him.' He said: 'What have you brought?' He said: 'Is that good?' I said: 'Yes, I am sure.' He said to the people: 'He brought us much wealth. If you want we shall count it or if you want we shall weigh it.'"

18. "Those who treasure up gold and silver and do not expend them in the way of God – give them the good news of a painful chastisement, the day they shall be heated in the fire of Gehenna and therewith their foreheads and sides and their backs shall be branded: 'This is the thing you treasured up for yourselves:, therefore, taste you now what you were treasuring'" (Sūra 9:35).

19. The traditions relating to them are well-known and there is no need to describe them in detail. See the volumes containing biographies of the Companion such as Ibn Abd al-Barr, الاستيعاب (*Comprehension*), Ibn al-Athīr, أسد الغابة (*Usd al-Ghāba*) (*Lion of the Forest*) and Ibn Hajar, الإصابة (*al-Isāba*) (*The Correct Answer*) as well as the historical works among others. It is not only a question of the accumulation of wealth but goes beyond that to include failure to observe Islamic values in the field of ethics: an incident of this kind is the murder of Malik ibn Nuwayra al-Tamīmī by Khālid ibn Walīd, using a false pretext of apostasy. He then imposed himself on al-Tamīmī's attractive widow, whom he was courting, without waiting for the legal delay or *istibra.'*

20. The book of al-Mawardi, أدب الدنيا و الدين (*adab al-dunya wa-l-dīn*) (*Literature of the World and of Religion*) is a good example of this tendency.

21. This is affirmed by the distinguished Swiss psychologist, Jean Piaget. Hishām Charabi

makes the same point in his work (published in Arabic), *The Patriarchal System and Backwardness in Arab Societies* (Beirut, 1993), pp. 62–3.

22. Al-Sarakhshi, شرح السير الكبير (*The Great Commentary on the Biographies and of Religion*) (Hyderabad, 1355/1936), vol. I, pp. 125–6. Sufyān al-Thawri relies on the following verses: "Who so commits aggression against you, do you commit aggression against him" (Sūra 2:191) and "Fight the unbelievers totally even as they fight you totally" (Sūra 9:36). Al-Sarakhshi corrects this viewpoint, saying that the order to engage in *jihād* and fighting was revealed progressively. The Prophet initially received the order to transmit the message and avoid the polytheists. Then he received the order to dialogue with them in the best possible way. Subsequently, he was authorised to fight them if they initiated hostilities. Then followed the command to fight outside of the sacred months, before being instructed simply to fight against them. Al-Sarakhshi expresses here the dominant interpretation justifying offensive war.

23. Al-Sarakhshi mentions the opinion of al-Awzā'i according to which "the Muslims are not permitted to carry out destructive acts in enemy territory because that constitutes disorder (*fasād*) and God does not like disorder". Al-Sarakhshi corrects this opinion saying: "If it is praiseworthy to construct, destruction is a motive for blame. But we say: since it is permitted to kill in order to reduce the power of the enemy – and this is the gravest of actions – it is all the more authorized to destroy buildings and cut down trees." شرح السير الكبير (*The Great Commentary on the Biographies*), vol. I, p. 35.

Institutionalised Islam

1. The allusion is to 'Umar ibn al-Khattāb.
2. See the present author's thesis, "Arab thought's reply to Christians", الفكر الإسلامي في الرد على النصارى', pp. 183–5.
3. Al-Tijāni, writing at the beginning of the second/eighth century in his رحلة (*Journey*) (Tunis, 1378/1958), p. 187, notes that "The inhabitants of Ghomrassen [in southern Tunisia] and the majority of those living in this mountainous region are Muslim only in name. None of them knows the name of the prayers, let alone how to pray in the approved manner. The same can be said of all the precepts of Islam. During the period we were there, we never heard a call to prayer and the voice of the muezzin was inaudible to us. I saw a place high up on their fortress that they term an oratory although the only person who prays is a stranger from Zaouara living among them ... they do not wash their dead nor do they pray over them. The daughter inherits nothing from her father."
4. Concerning these disorders of the fourth/tenth and fifth/eleventh centuries see Ibn al-Jawzi, المنظم (*A Categorical Collection of the History of the Nations*) (Beirut, 1992), vols 13–15.
5. See, for example, Ira M. Lapidus, "The Institutionalization of Early Islamic Societies" in Toby E. Huff and Wolfgang Schluchter (eds), *Max Weber and Islam* (New Brunswick and London, 1999), pp. 148–50.
6. The two angels who examine the dead in their graves as to the quality of their faith, questioning them about Muhammad. Both believers and non-believers are questioned. Their names do not appear in the Qur'an. Jewish traditions of a similar nature exist.

7. Caliph from 232/847 to 247/861.

8. Application of what is legally prescribed.

9. Sheikh Mahmūd Abū Rayya's book, شيخ المضيرة (*Shaikh al-Madhīra*) contains numerous accounts of this.

10. See Cl. Gilliot , "Portrait mythique d'Ibn 'Abbās", *Arabica*, XXXII, 1985, pp. 127–84.

11. In the well known tradition in which 'Umar ibn al Khattāb and al-Hurmuzān appear after the conquest of Persia, the vanquished al-Hurmuzān addresses the victorious 'Umar as follows: "We considered you, the Arabs, as no more than dogs." See, for example, al-Sarakhshi, شرح السيار الكبير (*The Great Commentary on the Biographies*) (Hyderabad, 1355/1937), vol. 1, p. 176.

12. Ibn Khaldoun, *al-Muqadimmah: An Introduction to History* (trans. Franz Rosenthal (Beirut, 1967–8), vol. I, p. 83.

13. See, for example, the use of the theme of the spider's web or that of the hatching of a dove's eggs in a cave where a fugitive has taken refuge while his enemies are pursuing him. These famous anecdotes which concern the Hegira and the expedition of 'Abdallah ibn Anīs appear in Al-Sarakhshi's شرح السيار الكبير (*The Great Commentary on the Biographies*) vol. I, p. 179. It would be worth making a detailed comparison with themes present in the cultures of the Near East.

14. Abū al Hasan al-'Amīrī, الأعلام بمناقب الإسلام, (*Guide to the Glories of Islam*) (Cairo, 1967), pp. 118–19.

15. Mohammed Abd al-Jabri, in his book, نقد العقل العربي (*A Critical Study of Arab Rationality*) maintains that the Islamic sciences acquired their definitive form at an early stage. However, there are substantial differences between the scholarly production of the second/eighth and third/ninth centuries of the Hegira and that of the three following centuries. Nor can one downplay the efforts of Muslim scholars in the first/seventh century and the second half of the second/eighth century on the grounds that this thought was nonexistent, given the lack of texts whose authors can be identified prior to the period of codification. Arab or Islamic thought (if it can be referred to in the singular form), developed and took form gradually. The first, obscure period determined its essential characteristics.

The Elaboration of Institutional Theory

1. It is regrettable that serious research on this subject is still non-existent. Abū Sari' Muhammad's اختلاف الصحابة أسبابه و اثاره في الفقه الإسلامي (*The Disagreements Among the Companions: Causes and Consequences in Muslim Fiqh* (Cairo, 1991), and other works of this kind are of very little use to the scholar.

2. Ibn Khaldoun, *The Muqadimmah: An Introduction to History,* trans. from the Arabic by Franz Rosenthal (Princeton, 1958), pp. 15–16.

3. Ibn Khaldoun, *The Muqadimmah*, vol. 1, pp. 55–7.

4. Ibn Khaldoun, *The Muqadimmah*, pp. 72–3.

5. Ibn Khaldoun, *The Muqadimmah*, p. 76.

6. Ibn Khaldoun, *The Muqadimmah*, vol. II, p. 462.

7. See Hunayda Hafsa, حضور النص - القرآني في المدو نة الكبرى (*The Qur'anic Text in the*

Mudawwana l-Kubrā), diplôme d'études approfondies (DEA), Faculty of Arts and Humanities, University of Manouba, 1999).

8. See M. Billig and D. Edwards, "La construction sociale de la mémoire", *La Recherche*, vol. 25, No. 267, juillet–aout 1994, p. 742. Frederick Bartlett, an English psychologist, has demonstrated that we process or modify the data that we receive before stocking it in our memory. Our memories are not mere copies of our perceptions. He found that people did not recall the exact words of a story, retaining them in a form of their own devising to which they add elements which were not originally present.

9. The Prophet's attitude to women can be cited, although he made concessions to Umar ibn al-Khattab over the latter's insistence that free women be veiled, as well as to the Quraysh concerning their custom of wife beating, less prevalent among the inhabitants of Medina.

10. See Jeanne Ladjili, *Histoire juridique de la Méditerranée: droit romain, droit musulman* (Tunis, 1990).

11. *Far' ع* فرع ("branch") علم الفروع (*Ilm al furū'*) is the science of applied *fiqh* or applied ethics.

12. Numerous editions exist of بداية المجتهد و نهاية المقتصد (*The Beginning of the Legist and the End of the Mediator*), for example, the 1385/1966 Cairo edition in two volumes. رحمة الأمة في اختلاف الأئمة (*The Compassion of the Community and the Divergence of the Spiritual Leaders*) by al-Dimashqi can be consulted in the second edition published in Cairo in 1386/1967.

13. Although the legislative and canonical dimension is less important in Christianity, there are similarities between Christian and Muslim jurists. The former speak of the "law" [*nomos* in Greek] of God" while the latter use the term شرع‌الله ("*Shar'allah*"). See, for example, Book IV of *The Canons of the Kings According to Makarios*, trans. Stefan Leder: *Das vierte Buch des Kanones der Koenige aus der sammlung des Makarios* (Frankfurt am Main, 1985), p. 30. Many of the canons contained in this book resemble Islamic juridical regulations.

14. *Musāqāh*, مساقاة contract for the lease of a plantation limited to one crop period.

15. Abu Hayyān et-Tawhīdi wonders, in disgust: "Who authorized a particular judge to declare that relations with a particular woman are illicit while another judge says the contrary? The same is true of judgments concerning money and life itself. One judge's word means death, while another prevents this. They disagree in this shameful way, make arbitrary judgments, and yield to their passions and desires." الهوامل الشوامل (*al-hawāmil was as-shawāmil*) (*Rambling and Comprehensive Questions*) (Cairo, 1370/1951), p. 153.

16. Rāzi, المحصول (*al-Mahsūl*), vol. III, pp. 220–1. Unevenness of duties and obligations reflects a discriminatory outlook which almost dehumanises the person of different sex or colour. See, for example, the reproaches directed against the Mu'tazalites by Ibn al-Rawandi because they maintained, in al-Rawandi's words that "the blacks are able to write poetry and compose letters". See فضيحة المعتزلة (*The Scandal of the Mu'tazila*) (Beyrouth/Paris, 1975–7), p. 131.

17. Abu Talib al-Makkī, قوت القلوب (*Nourishment for the Heart*) (Cairo, 1991), vol. II, p. 97. One may consult the chapter that he devotes to "The 'ulamā' of this world and the 'ulamā' of the world to come: condemnation of the 'ulamā' of evil who consume this world by

Islam

their sciences", pp. 94–104. The position of al-Ghazali in جواهر القرآن (*Jewels of the Qur'an*) (Beirut, 1977) is close to that of al-Makkī.

18. Ibn Rushd, somewhat curiously, justifies his position among the *ahl al-burhān* ("adepts of proof") by a distinctive interpretation of verse 7 of the Sūra *al-Imran*: "It is He who sent down upon thee the Book wherein are verses clear that are the Essence of the Book, and others ambiguous. As for those in whose hearts is swerving, they follow the ambiguous part, desiring dissension, and desiring its interpretation; and none knows its interpretation save only God. And those firmly rooted in knowledge say, 'We believe in it; all is from our Lord'; yet none remembers, but men possessed of minds." When he discusses al-Ghazali's accusation that philosophers were infidels, he deals with three questions: the eternal existence of the world; God's ignorance of particulars; and the resurrection of the body. He says: "We have interpretations that must only be expounded to scholars of interpretation, those who are grounded in knowledge, because it is best, in our view, to stand by the Word of God: 'those firmly rooted in knowledge.'" He divides people into "practitioners of oratorical argumentation" (the majority group) and "practitioners of dialectical interpretation" (meaning the *kalām* scholars), and "practitioners of certain interpretation", namely "the wise". This is what he says about the abovementioned verse of the Qur'an: "Therefore it must be clearly stated, concerning the exterior meaning of the verse, that it is obscure, and that God alone understands it. This word of God should be considered here: 'None knows its interpretation save God Himself.'" See فصل المقال (*Fasl al-maqāl*) (*On the Harmony of Religions and Philosophy*) (Beirut, 1961), pp. 38–9, 53, and the present author's article, في ذكرى أبي وليد ("In memory of Ibn Rushd"), in the review رحاب المعرف (*Rihāb al-maʿarifa*) Tunis, No. 3, May–June 1998, pp. 18–22.

19. See "Al-Kindi's letter to Mu'tasim Billah concerning the first philosophy", رسالة الكندي إلى المعتصم بالله في الفلسفة الأولى, in *Al Kindi's Philosophical Letters*, رسائل الكندي الفلسفية pp. 103–4.

20. See Abū Hasan al ʿAmiri, الإعلام بمناقب الإسلام (*Instruction in the Glories of Islam*), (Cairo, 1967), p. 154.

21. Al-Wancharīsī, المعيار (*al-Miʿyār*) "gauge" or "measurement" (Beirut, 1981), vol. II, p. 508. Certain *fuqahā'* were opposed to imitation in such matters. According to Ibn Rushd (the grandfather of the philosopher) "God created all beings, constituting them in peoples and tribes, separating them from one another and giving them different dress and aspects. No one should abandon these attires and aspects willed by the Creator, and adopt others, because they are part of what is permitted for humankind." الفتاوى (*al-Fatāwa*) (*Legal Opinions*) (Beirut, 1987), vol. II, p. 964. Al-Shātibi observes that "if one calls every change in customs blameworthy innovation, then one should do the same for everything that was not the prevailing custom in the early days of Islam in the areas of food, drink, dress, language and so on. Such an idea is to be rejected because certain customs vary according to time, place, and name. Those who are different from the Arabs who knew the Companions and imitated their habits, would not take them as examples. That is reprehensible." See *al-Iʿtisām* ("preservation") الاعتصام (Beirut, 1988), vol. II, pp. 77–88.

22. See Abdelhamīd al-Harāma, القصيدة الأندلسية خلال القرن الثامن الهجري (*The Andalusian Poem in the Eighth Century of the Hegira* (Tripoli, 1996)), vol. I, p. 279.

174